PENGUIN ANANDA

BUDDHA IN LOVE

Geetanjali Pandit is an alumna of XLRI (Xavier Institute of Management), Jamshedpur, and Lesley University, Cambridge, USA. While studying abroad, she had the unique distinction of working for the legendary economist and diplomat John Kenneth Galbraith. Her career in human resources spans over twenty-two years, during which time she has been the chief human resources officer for the India Today Group, the chief people officer for Zee Media Corporation Limited and played a global role in employer branding and hospitality practices at Oberoi Hotels and Resorts (EIH Limited). Her work in creating positive social attitudinal transformation has led to her becoming the Rex Karmaveer Global Fellow 2023–24. An articulate speaker and incisive thinker, she has written two books on career management and several articles in *Economic Times*, *Financial Express* and *DNA*.

She credits her success entirely to the application of the Buddha's teachings to her life and to her work. Geetanjali is now a bestselling author and content creator.

T0290369

Celebrating 35 Years of
Penguin Random House India

ADVANCE PRAISE FOR THE BOOK

'*Buddha in Love* redefines what it means to have great partnerships. You will never think about the quest for love and relationships the same way again. A must-read!'—Shibani Kashyap, singer

'Geetanjali expertly weaves spirituality into modern dating. She allows readers to learn the Buddha's lessons by sharing her deeply personal story. If you want to find a semblance of peace in the everyday madness of relationships, this is the book for you'—Natasha Chandel, Indo-American-Canadian screenwriter, comedian and host, *Kinda Dating*

'Geetanjali Pandit is an amazingly gifted writer who transports us through real-life scenarios. She speaks with candour and complete authenticity about her life, trauma and healing. Highly recommend this unusual and wonderful book'—Nasir Abdullah, model and actor

'As society grapples with algorithmically mediated romances, *Buddha in Love* serves as a timely call, urging us to examine whether our modern conceptions of love can be enriched, or perhaps even redefined, by the ancient wisdom of the Buddha. The work challenges us to strive for neither renunciation nor hedonistic excess but for a love that truly befits our humanness. It is, in essence, a work that asks us to walk the Middle Path with grace'—Rajiv Mehrotra, author and documentary film-maker

BUDDHA in LOVE

Building Healthy and Lasting Partnerships

GEETANJALI PANDIT

PENGUIN

ANANDA

An imprint of Penguin Random House

PENGUIN ANANDA

USA | Canada | UK | Ireland | Australia
New Zealand | India | South Africa | China | Singapore

Penguin Ananda is part of the Penguin Random House group of companies
whose addresses can be found at global.penguinrandomhouse.com

Published by Penguin Random House India Pvt. Ltd
4th Floor, Capital Tower 1, MG Road,
Gurugram 122 002, Haryana, India

Penguin
Random House
India

First published in Penguin Ananda by Penguin Random House India 2023

Copyright © Geetanjali Pandit 2023

All rights reserved

10 9 8 7 6 5 4 3 2 1

The views and opinions expressed in this book are the author's own and the
facts are as reported by her which have been verified to the extent possible,
and the publishers are not in any way liable for the same.

ISBN 9780143457787

Typeset in Sabon by Manipal Technologies Limited, Manipal
Printed at Replika Press Pvt. Ltd, India

This book is sold subject to the condition that it shall not, by way of trade
or otherwise, be lent, resold, hired out, or otherwise circulated without the
publisher's prior consent in any form of binding or cover other than that in
which it is published and without a similar condition including this condition
being imposed on the subsequent purchaser.

www.penguin.co.in

MIX
Paper from
responsible sources
FSC® C016779

To Gautama Buddha and his eternal teachings

*To Nichiren Daishonin, Dr Daisaku Ikeda,
eternal mentor and the Sangha of the Soka Gakkai*

To Manu and the Sangha of our family

CONTENTS

INTRODUCTION

Was it playing *ghar-ghar*, the make-believe game of home, family and innocence? Was it the stereotype of my upbringing? Was it the stereotype of the world of Mills & Boons books that I immersed myself in from the age of 11?

I don't really know but the idea of the imperative of being married and having a family, having children, seized my mind from a young and very impressionable age. My growing years were marked with disturbances at home and the need for my own family grew stronger. I don't exactly recall when it tipped over into neediness. But surely it did.

Finding love became the big quest of my life. I looked for romantic love and someone to cherish me from my teen years. Yet, there was an immaturity in tackling my own emotions, and I never cherished myself. Time became unforgiving of my wrong choices and acquainted me with its offspring, regret. The incompletions left a painful imprint on my mind and life. And I started feeling less than others around me. Less than a socially stamped 'normal'.

Was it my robust Punjabi spirit that kept me going and always kept me hopeful of finding love? Was it just a natural in-built doggedness? I refused to give up on my dreams even with the passage of time and years. Even decades. And irrespective of what the voices outside said. Yes, it was painful to hear them and their harsh barbs. But somehow I had the strength of mind to hold on my dreams for my life.

I had to heal and to let go of the past, with its many mistakes and downright abuse. When Vunita Sarrin introduced me to the practice of Nichiren Daishonin's teachings, it became my watershed moment. I learnt to let go and to forgive. I learnt to heal. The writings of Dr Daisaku Ikeda and the support of the Sangha prodded me to reflect, to change and to become empowered in living my life. I learnt that the first and most vital relationship that needs to fall into place is the one we have with ourselves. We are priceless sparkling treasure. When we learn the skill of cherishing ourselves, a world of possibilities unfolds.

Possibilities unfold because we change. As did I. The outside is a true mirror, capturing and reflecting all that is taking place within. The harshness of my circumstances forced me to revise my worldview; compelled me to change from within. I had to work hard on myself and staring at the mirror of my own life, acknowledge that much was amiss. I was harbouring anger within, blaming my parents and others for all that had gone wrong in my life. I lacked clarity and conviction. Somehow, somewhere I had bought into all that the world had to say and only chaos ruled.

Once again that doggedness came to the rescue. True, I lacked clarity and conviction. Yet, I did not lack honesty nor courage. I was determined to find a way out. It was only complete forgiveness of those who had hurt and damaged me that allowed for an equally complete healing of my life. I soared free. And perhaps, with that forgiveness, with a new calmness and a newfound sense of responsibility for my life and my decisions, I truly changed my karma.

Now when I look back on the incompletions of my past years, I only see lessons I have gained from. Lessons that helped me to grow up. To simply grow. Yet, I have found myself wishing that life lessons had not been so hard or so harsh. And wishing still that someone had guided me differently.

It was chance (or luck?) that I did not fall by the wayside or that I did not end up taking my own life. A little spark of hope kept me from that final step, from giving up on my dreams so violently.

Buddha In Love is the expression of my hope that my readers don't have to gaze back on time and feel that life could have been better . . . if only.

'If only', we say, 'if only I had someone who could help me understand life and relationships better, someone who could help me find love. Someone who understands me and does not judge my desires and unique situation in life. Someone I could turn to and seek counsel from. Someone who could help me to slow down for a moment and think for myself. Someone who could help me attract and sustain healthy, loving relationships. Someone that could help in living my "happily ever after".'

Buddha in Love is that someone, that something that can help each one of its readers find love and build relationships. To heal from disappointments and heartbreak. To fulfill that longing for creating the life that we desire. For that warm, loving and intimate relationship with a special someone.

Come, be a part of my journey. Come, fall in love . . .

A TRAGEDY UNFOLDS QUIETLY

> '"He abused me, he beat me
> He defeated me, he robbed me":
> The hatred of those who harbour
> such thoughts is not appeased'
>
> —Buddha (*The Dhammapada*)

That night, I lay in a pool of my own blood. As the night before. And the night after.

I knew I had to escape this sham marriage somehow. Anyhow.

I was traumatized. Cold and numbed to the core of my soul. Shrivelling away under the weight of my life choices. I had already demonstrated a poor ability to stick to commitments and manage my emotions, to manage life well. Unable to make the right decisions in the matter of choosing a life partner.

Driven by the problems of my own personality and those of my family, I was in a state of endless reaction—to life and to situations; to the things in my hands; to the ones out of my control. I had become used to reacting unreasonably. Reaction upon reaction. Mistake upon mistake. Each one took me a step closer to drowning in the abyss of misery.

After all, it was my inability to manage my own emotions that had landed me in this mess. Insecurity and anxiety had always been my companions, as far back as I could remember. Perhaps it had to do with growing up in a privileged yet dysfunctional family with a hostile older sibling, a supremely successful father who, in his mid-50s, developed bipolar disorder, and a nurturing mother who only wanted what was best for me. Each of them played an integral role in making me who I was and shaping the best and the worst of me. And for the better part of life, the worst was winning.

My brother's hostility in words and actions made me feel unsafe. Our lack of money was a constant reminder of my father's spotless integrity as well as his stubborn lack of worldly understanding. The lurking threat of an insecure future. A constant fear of what the future would hold. As I botched one element of my life after another, my record of failures was growing. Beginning with my failure to qualify for the civil service. It was just the first of many attempts to succeed. At life. In life. The first of many attempts to escape my own circumstances.

Ironically, even though a police officer's child, I experienced life through a prison of circumstances. My own lack of understanding of life and the huge anxiety I experienced were the bars that held me firmly in place. I was imprisoned by my own limitations and my inability to break free of circumstances. It was irony at its best.

Was this my karma? Was this fate? Was I destined to suffer through my circumstances? What would it take to break free and make a fresh start?

That's all I ever wanted. To break free and make a fresh start.

I did break free for a bit. My selection for the MBA at the Xavier Labour Relations Institute, or Xavier School of Management as it is now known (XLRI), was the first bit of freedom I experienced. It was a chance to live on my own and not suffer the family circumstances.

But then the anxious me, the emotional me and the immature me went and screwed it up. Academically. Romantically. Royally.

At XLRI, I failed miserably in every possible way. I failed even before I could take off for a better life. I had loved and lost. Unable to handle my own emotions and unsupported in that decision by those close to me, I called off my wedding a mere fortnight before the event.

Poor grades were forever stamped on my academic career. Heartbreak was stamped forever on my heart. And just like stamps on a passport, these were twin visas to battered emotions and an impaired ability to take the right decisions.

There was more to follow. My mother's pancreatic cancer took only four months to progress from diagnosis to her death. My father was 70 and suffering from depression. My brother returned home and appeared to be unleashing the familiar hostility upon my dad and me again. Crises heaped upon crises, and there was no time to heal. No time to hit pause on this LP of misery. I had to just bear it and go through it. Sometimes breathing and sometimes not.

This time, I sought escape in marriage. I thought it would be the easiest way out. Perhaps it would answer my deepest desire and my intense longing to have a normal family life. A normal life.

Would it?

Spurred by my emotional desperation and a deep-rooted need to find security through money and position, I married the wrong man. What was I thinking? The regret ran through my veins like the fiercest acid. Erosive. Unalterable. I could simply not recover from the blows that were dealt to me, one after another, by a fate that was brutal and sadistic. I remembered the lines from a class in English Lit, a lifetime ago: 'As flies to wanton boys are we to the gods; They kill us for their sport'.

Perhaps each link in this chain of endless misery was crafted by my inability to make smart decisions. To decide from a core of belief and calmness in life. I carried an unshakeable sense that life was out of control. Year after year, we moved from one crisis to another. As I was the youngest and somehow willing to step up and take responsibility, I was mostly around my parents when these crises were both being created and dealt with. I was tired of it all even before I turned 22.

Each mistake whipped up my insecurities and weakened my judgement. Each step was born of my desperation to find a family, create a family and have a home. To find refuge from life's problems. To find a safe harbour. To lead a normal life. My mother was my anchor, but she was gone in a matter of months. I was left alone. Bereft of her love and her assurance that life would someday be okay and that all would be well. I pined for my mother's love. Perhaps any mother's love. I ached to be hugged and to be told that it would all fall into place. And that I would live happily ever after. Someday. Somehow. Magically.

The marriage ended, and it ended soon. Within just forty-five days of its start. The abuse was subtle and brutal, embedding itself into my body and my soul. There was an intent to humiliate. To control. I was off-kilter throughout. The same family, in their interactions with my father prior to the wedding, had lavished a whole lot of compliments and appreciation. It proved to be a huge charade. 'The transformation from Dr Jekyll to Mr Hyde was amazing,' I thought to myself through the mist of helpless misery.

And for the first time ever, I experienced actual fear. A fear that turned my bones to jelly and my insides to liquid. Sitting on the pot, I would pee for an hour sometimes, the fear running out of my body and making me urinate uncontrollably. I understood for the first time the helplessness that can be inflicted on one person by another. I felt like prey—vulnerable and exposed. And equally terrified.

Perhaps it was this fear and the helpless terror that birthed an intense loathing. For the first time in my life, I learned to hate someone from the depths of my soul. Soon, rage would be added to this mix of fear and hatred.

Those forty-five days were a mistake from start to finish. There were hints to stop calling my father and one or two of my friends. To follow and obey the rules of the new family. I was ignorant of the symptoms of systemic domestic abuse. I only knew and accepted the enormity of the mistake I had made.

Escape was not easy, but I managed it with the help of a close friend. Only to step into a morass of character assassination. And as the brutal, senseless character assassination stepped up, I got more isolated than ever. Just when I could have done with greater support from the extended family, they bought into the vicious lies.

At the age of 73, my father was a shadow of his powerful former self. His once strong and fit body was wrecked by the rapid cycles of bipolar depression and all the medication. And crisis after crisis within the family had left him hollowed out physically, emotionally and financially.

No, my father had not forced me into this arranged marriage. But a few days after the informal engagement ceremony of *roka*, when I wanted to opt out, my father's accusations and his sarcasm about my past indecision kept me in the orbit of what would prove to be the most disastrous decision. Oh, if only I could turn back time and undo my mistakes. If only life would move into rewind mode. If only I could get another chance. If only . . .

Emotions and thoughts swirled in a jumbled mess. Again and again. Increasing my feelings of helplessness. How would I ever emerge from the shambles that my life had turned into? I was without a job, without resources, without money, without support and without friends. I was alone and without hope.

Perhaps I would soon be without life itself. I could choose to end my life.

Would I have the courage to?

'Whatever harm a foe may do to a foe, or a hater to another hater, a wrongly directed mind may do one harm far exceeding these.'

—The Buddha (*The Dhammapada*)

A CHANCE MEETING

suicide

noun

the intentional taking of one's own life

destruction of one's own interests or prospects

I had already destroyed so much through my own stupidity and shortsightedness. It was a lack of understanding of life. I worked against myself, against my own interests. It was strange, but true: I was unwittingly my own enemy. I had succeeded in destroying my prospects. All that was left was to destroy my life. To intentionally finish my life, as life itself was finished for me.

I was back at my father's place, avoiding the neighbours who had seen me whisked away as a radiant bride a mere forty-five days ago. At the age of 33, I was now a soon-to-be divorcee. Unemployed. Life had been reduced to survival each day, and there was no fight left in me to even crawl out of the abyss I found myself in.

I had little hope that there would be some miracle from up above. Had the gods given up on me, or had I given up on them?

I trudged from job interview to job interview, mumbling about personal circumstances and an impending divorce. It was difficult, if not impossible, to explain my circumstances to anyone. I could offer no explanations, no excuses. It simply was my truth then.

Health was becoming a big concern for both my ageing father and me. Dad had aged beyond imagination in a matter of months. He was supporting himself, my brother and now me on his government pension. I was trying my best to get a job. 'Any bloody job would do,' I thought to myself. It didn't have to match up to my academic credentials or the MBA degree from XLRI.

Is it any wonder that, in this wretched and miserable state, I caught myself thinking about ending my life?

Divorce would happen, and I could not expect my father to pay the lawyers. Perhaps it was time to sell my mother's jewellery. I had inherited a little bit of gold and about Rs 10 lakh from my mother. And held on to it even through my American sojourn, working four jobs at any given time to pay my way through the bit of the master's course that I had managed to complete.

The healing I experienced during that sojourn was all undone by the sordid mess of subsequent events and the most disastrous decision of marriage to the wrong person. Or was it for the wrong reasons? If I were to be honest about my reasons, I knew, at a gut level, that CP was simply wrong for me. I was marrying him for financial security. I was marrying him, hoping for maternal affection from his mother. I was hoping that marriage would fill the many voids in my life and become the answer to all my problems.

Exhaustion overwhelmed me one evening. Yet another job interview had ended on the much hated note of, 'We are meeting other candidates'. I knew it marked the tombstone of my hopes of landing one more opportunity to find work, to find meaningful employment and to earn the money that I so desperately needed. Driving through the intense heat of the June afternoon, my hopes as scorched as Delhi's roads, I knew I could not carry on much longer.

For my parents' sake and for the sake of my family's reputation, I would have to resort to an ending that appeared to be an accident. Perhaps an evening walk . . . a walk I could choose not to return from. These thoughts possessed me even as I parked my battered Maruti 800 and dragged myself up the stairs to the modest apartment I shared with my father. A wash with the hot water that naturally gushed through the pipes in the scorching heat of summer and ten minutes of throwing myself on the bed under the old, heavy and ineffective fan were not enough to break the desperation or the intent to finish it all.

My father knocked on the door to my room. We had run out of groceries and veggies, and he needed some medicines too. He kept refilling his prescription from five years earlier, ducking the doctor and additional consultation fees.

I hastily put the few currency notes he gave me into the back pocket of my jeans, got a few sturdy cloth bags from the kitchen, and dragged my weary and aching body down the stairs.

While at the vegetable market, I didn't feel the nimble fingers dip into my back pocket nor notice the swift dash of the young boy away from the cart. It was only when I put my hand in my pocket to pay the vendor that I realized that I had been robbed.

The disbelief quickly turned into anger. All the miseries of life woke to a howling rage. And just as swiftly, the rage transformed into abject misery, leaving me shaking and shuddering. Tears fell. Anguish ripped at my heart.

I don't know how long I stood there. Was it an aeon or a matter of minutes? I only know that the trance was broken by a cool touch—a gentle tap on my shoulder. Turning towards it, I found my gaze resting on the calmest countenance I had ever seen. A tranquil smile, one that combined both great power and great poise, lit up the face of the young man standing there. The sounds of the busy bazaar, the noise off the road, and the smells of the market just vanished. Just faded away.

I studied the young man. He was simply dressed and carried himself with an air of calm confidence. His regular denims, cool white T-shirt and open-toed sandals looked crisp and fresh even in the sweltering heat.

'Yes?' I croaked through the tears and the misery.

'Hi,' he responded in a wonderfully smooth baritone. His voice was mellow yet strong. So caught up was I in that extraordinary voice that I nearly missed what he was saying: 'Here, I got your money back from the young man who had taken it.' I gazed down at the notes lying on his open palm. 'Go ahead and complete your work.'

'Oh! Thank you. Thank you so very much,' I managed to squeeze out.

'Not at all. I saw what was happening and am glad to help. After all, we have friends in common,' he replied calmly with a fabulous smile.

'Friends in common?' I was confused and beginning to feel a bit alarmed.

'Yes, Rajeev Churamani and Vuneeta Sarrin are our common friends, and I have been wanting to meet you for some time.'

I felt a bit reassured and a bit more at ease with this striking stranger. Hurrying to complete my chores, I hefted my filled shopping bags and completed the payments to the fruit seller and the vegetable vendor even as the extraordinary stranger fell into step with me. Belatedly, I realized that he had said he had been wanting to meet me for some time. Why? Just who was he? The reassurance I had started experiencing melted away like an ice cube on Delhi's roads in midsummer. Again, a feeling of near panic surfaced.

Striving to sound calm and at ease, I asked him, 'Why have you been wanting to meet me?' I stole a look at him from the corner of my eyes.

'I can be a friend and guide you, perhaps, in how to be happy. I have helped many others in similar situations. I have also helped those in far worse situations,' he said gently.

'Far worse situations,' I thought to myself. Surely there was very little that was far worse than what had unfolded in my life. Yet, somehow, his presence was having a calming effect on me. I was, in fact, feeling more settled than I had moments ago. There was something about him—a poise and a calmness—that was beyond my experience.

'So, how you will help me?' I asked and suspiciously added, 'What are you expecting in return for your help?'

'I suggest that we go somewhere and get something cold to drink so that we can discuss solutions to your problems and get you started on them. As for what I want, I want you to help others in turn, when you can. Just pay it forward when life becomes easier and better. When it all falls into place.'

Somehow, I found myself agreeing to have a drink with him.

As he fell into step beside me, the man turned to look at me. 'Oh, by the way,' he said, 'my name is Gautam.'

A PRINCE IS BORN

The Indian subcontinent has always been large and wedge-shaped. Water surrounds this land on three sides, with the snowy peaks of the mighty Himalayas to its north.

For centuries before and after the Buddha's birth, the land was fertile, and even the poorest could access food and the bounty of the many jungles. There was no scarcity of food or land for cultivation.

In the Buddha's time, large areas of north India were forest-covered and the people who lived in the many villages on the borders of the forest came across lions, elephants, deer and rhinos.

Such was the nature of the land where the Buddha was born, lived and taught. The canvas for the Buddha's life was north-central India. It was largely the Gangetic basin, with a vast, flat and fertile plain through which majestic rivers flowed. The mighty Ganges moved through its journey of 1600 miles, giving birth to countless others. The Gangetic plain was becoming and had become the centre of Indic civilization.

History reminds us that there were three distinct seasons at this time. The hot but dry summer, the rainy season when all would come to a halt, and the winter with its cool days and freezing cold nights. Fruit, rice, barley, sesame, millet and wheat were produced for consumption and, increasingly, for trade.

Sanskrit and Pali texts refer to this land as Jambudvipa, or the Land of the Rose Apple. Jambu is the name of the tree and its fruit (the rose apple) and *dvipa* is the continent or land.

The Brahmanism prevalent at the time believed in one supreme God and lesser (almost human) gods that governed some aspects of nature. And so there was the fire god Agni, the rain god Indra, the god of death Yama, the sun god Surya and many others. All of them were pleased or appeased through rituals, offerings and sacrifices. The common man feared the wrath of the gods because it would result in drought, floods or illness. Fear ruled the mind, and often, religion was interpreted to ensure that fear continued. The fear led to continuity in tradition. It also meant that a certain section of society was kept in business.

All these rituals, offerings and sacrifices needed the caste of Brahmins to act as intermediaries because only they knew the prayers and could conduct the rituals to please the gods and protect the common person from the harm that the anger of the gods could bring.

Just like today, there was a movement for great change in religion and in society. This great change started unfolding before the birth of the Buddha and, of course, continued with him. It was the age of challenge. The old ways were being turned upside down and questioned by a few. A new socio-religious thought was emerging—new thoughts, new ideas and a new spiritual understanding.

India, or Jambudvipa, was not to become a single political entity until the time and rule of King Ashoka (nearly 220 years in the future from the Buddha's time), and so at the time of the Buddha, India was a collection of independent states (called *janpads*) and large kingdoms (called *mahajanpads*). These states and kingdoms often fought with each other for political gain and supremacy. A significant part of life was played out in urban centres and cities. Six cities emerged and vied with each other for trade and industry in the north: Savatthi, Saketa, Kosambi, Varanasi, Rajagriha and Champa. New trade routes were being made and linked. The two new monarchies of Kosala and Magadha were modern, aggressive and efficient in their administration.

The cities were fast-paced and exciting to be in. Their streets were undoubtedly crowded with elephants carrying merchandise and serving as the primary transport for the traders and their goods. There were chariots and horses that belonged to the warriors. The glamour and shocking, modern ways of the cities were very different from the simple village life. Here there was theatre, gambling, dancing and even prostitution. The taverns lent themselves to rowdy entertainment and lively meetings.

The caste system was firmly in place. The Brahmins occupied the first rung as the priests and officiators of all rituals governing human life, from birth to death and even after. Kshatriyas occupied second place, with all rulers, warriors and the governing class belonging to this caste. The merchants and traders were the Vaishyas, while the craftsmen and those engaged in hard physical labour formed the last element of this social fabric. Sanskrit was the language of the priests. Pali was the language of the common man (in this region).

Voices were heard questioning the acceptance of the priestly caste as the keepers of traditions and scriptures. The status quo was being questioned. Power was passing to the Vaishyas, the merchants in the new social reality. A new urban class was being formed in the *janpads* and *mahajanpads*, the cities. Forests were being cleared for cultivation. More settlers around the cities and rich agricultural land shifted the population, making it denser in those areas. Aggressive trade and the economic boom were creating social prosperity and greed. Competition was the new reality of life. Tradition was under scrutiny, and its edges were crumbling.

Sakya was a small, semi-independent republic. Its capital was the city of Kapilavastu. The clan of Sakyas belonged to the Kshatriya, or warrior caste. They had a well-deserved reputation for hot-headedness and family pride.

The Sakyas, as befitted a republic, had a council, or *sabha*, made up of warriors of the tribe. All the councilmen were required to contribute to the *sabha*. Some contributed their physical skill with arms, and others shared their wisdom and experience, or wealth. This *sabha* met regularly, settled disputes among the citizens, and acted both as a governing council and a court of law.

The foremost councilman was elected as the head, or *mukhiya*, and acted as the ruler of the Sakyas. The selection of the *mukhiya* depended on various criteria, ranging from strength and courage in battle to wealth and riches of land and cattle, and also included wisdom and the skill of conflict resolution.

Suddhodana, whose name means 'pure grain' or 'pure rice', fulfilled these requirements and ruled the Sakyas for many years. He was married to two sisters. His wives were Mahamaya (the mother of the Buddha) and Maha Prajapati Gotami.

The Sakyas, whatever their original numbers, went through the cycle of ascension and decline. They are remembered today only because of one of their clansmen, the Buddha.

The boy child was born in this Sakya tribe (which led to his being called Sakyamuni, or the sage (*muni*) of the Sakyas later on). His family name was Gautama. Most historical references post the Great Enlightenment refer to him as Gautama or Tathagata. Found both in Sanskrit and Pali, Tathagata is one of the ten honourable titles of the Buddha and means one who has arrived from and into the realm of truth, one who observes things exactly as they are and who perceives the true nature of all things.

Omens pertaining to Siddhartha's birth and his eventual transformation into an enlightened one started before his conception. His mother, Mahamaya, dreamed of the Four Guardians of the Four Corners of the Land. She also dreamed of a beautiful white elephant, bearing in his trunk a white lotus. In the dream, this elephant touched her right side and entered her body.

The boy was born under a tree in Lumbini, Nepal, possibly the home of his maternal side. Mahamaya was travelling to be with her parents and kinsmen at the time of delivery, as was customary. Mahamaya passed away a few days after giving birth. The boy was lovingly raised by his maternal aunt, Maha Prajapati.

Following tradition and, as is customary, the naming ceremony was held. Here, the child was named Siddhartha. Interestingly, the meaning of 'Siddhartha' is 'accomplishment' or 'achievement of a goal'. His birth was certainly the achievement of the goal of having an heir—an important and vital goal for Suddhodana and the tribe itself.

On this occasion, eight soothsayers or astrologers were present among other Brahmins. Of these eight, seven foresaw that the child would become either a powerful king (chakravartin raja or universal monarch in the prophecy) or a buddha (an enlightened one). It would all depend on his experiences and his choices. The eighth, however, by the name of Kondana, predicted that he would definitely become a buddha. This same Kondana was, much later, among the first five disciples of the Buddha.

Then the prince's anxious father asked, 'What will my son see that will be the cause of his forsaking household life?'

'O King, your son will witness the Four Signs—a man worn out by age, a sick man, a dead body and an ascetic or *muni*,' came the answer.

Suddhodana vowed that he would protect his son from these sights, as he did not wish him to renounce the world. He fully intended for his newborn son to fulfil the other part of the prophecy and become the ruler of the world. Most certainly, the father wanted his son to be safe and to grow up to shoulder the responsibilities of the tribe and the kinsmen.

He now needed to ensure that Siddhartha would be protected from these realities of life and to keep him focused on what needed to be done for the tribe and the seat that he would inherit. Suddhodana was to remain troubled by this prediction for the next three decades. Even with all possible means and precautions, the father did not succeed in changing the course of his son's life.

'Gotama's pleasure palace is a striking image of a mind in denial. As long as we persist in closing our minds and hearts to the universal pain, which surrounds us on all sides, we remain locked in an undeveloped version of ourselves, incapable of growth and spiritual insight.

—Karen Armstrong in *Buddha*

MIRROR, MIRROR ON THE WALL

A DIM UNDERSTANDING DAWNS THAT MY LIFE IS MY REFLECTION

No one saves us but ourselves.
No one can and no one may.
We ourselves must walk the path.

—The Buddha

Even as Gautam and I fell into step and headed towards my ancient car, I felt out of sync. There was something unreal about walking off with this stranger, despite our common friends. And did he really mean it? Could he truly help me? How would he? I was, by no means, fully convinced or at ease. Yet, my desperation with my situation drove me on.

Gautam walked well, loose-limbed and at a pace that appeared neither fast nor slow. He was quiet and seemed to be deep in thought. Given his calm expression, his thoughts certainly appeared more pleasing than mine, I thought morosely. My thoughts were jumping all over, right from my anxiety over his identity and my safety in walking off with him and the puzzle of where to go with him for that cooling drink he had mentioned.

A short drive later, we were at Noida's Sector 37 main gate, just past Army Public School. I started feeling more at ease. The band of fear and anxiety loosened. I breathed a bit more freely and easily. This was familiar territory, after all. I had been living here with my father since 1999. As if sensing my thoughts, Gautam turned to me with a smile and said, 'Since you are familiar with this place, please suggest where we can sit and talk comfortably.'

There was something charming about Gautam. His ease with himself struck me even through my miasma of misery and anxiety. 'Let us head towards the Tea Shoppe,' I heard myself say. 'We can sit there comfortably and talk over a glass or two of cold peach tea.'

The Tea Shoppe was at once a connoisseur's delight with its collection of various teas straight from plantations, and yet it had all the warmth and charm of a *nukkad waali chai ki dukaan*.

Holding our glasses of cold peach tea, we sat on a well-placed bench, away from all those thronging the shop for their fix of cold teas and sandwiches. The evening was warm but bearable, and I just hoped that the mosquitoes would keep away. I could finally do away with the feelings of unease and just accept this time out with this stranger. With my mind made up and clarity about where to head, I felt more sorted about it all.

Rousing myself, I turned to Gautam and asked, 'So, Gautam, how do you think you can help me? And what exactly is the help you are going to give me? What will it do for me?'

Gautam was quiet. He was clearly mulling over something. And then that lovely masculine voice flowed over me, soothing places I didn't even know were hurting. 'I can help you to help yourself, GP.'

Somehow, on the way to the Tea Shoppe, I assumed that this mysterious, exciting stranger's offer of help would bring about a magical change. The child in me had perhaps never stopped hoping for a fairy godmother with a magic wand. The one who would somehow miraculously show up and rescue me.

And how could I help myself? Surely, if I had any capacity to help myself, it would have happened by now. I only had the Midas touch in reverse. These thoughts raced through my mind, but my words formed slowly. I said, 'If I could help myself, Gautam, do you think I would have been in this sorry situation? I don't exactly enjoy feeling miserable. I don't think anyone likes to suffer, feel hopeless about their life or feel sick about themselves. No one likes not having things turn out the way they have longed for, even worked for or for life to not be normal in even a single aspect.'

As I paused, I could see Gautam mulling over each line of my outburst. There was understanding and compassion in his next words to me: 'Eventually, only you can help yourself, GP. And when you resolve to work to help yourself, you will discover many things about yourself. You will find your own strength and wisdom. You will discover your ability to be happy in life.'

The depths of misery that I was steeped in made his words feel out of place. Happiness? Where was this happiness? When would I experience the feeling of being whole again? My growing-up years and family circumstances were so unique that I could not even describe what they had been like. How could I articulate my longing for my own home, for a normal family and a normal life?

Perhaps the seed had been sown in the disturbing circumstances of my childhood and adolescence. Misery upon misery had been compounded by my history of childhood illnesses that turned into hormonal distress and PCOD. The family stress had heaped on more misery yet.

Mom's death had left me bereft of feeling normal. She had been my family. Being motherless had intensified my desire and need for a loving man by my side and my own nest.

My thoughts were black with regret. I had taken so many wrong decisions in the matter of love, relationships and marriage—strangely, the one area that I wanted the most to work out! What I wanted the most, with the greatest intensity, appeared jinxed and out of reach.

My anguish must have reflected even as I said, 'My ability to be happy is zero. I am nothing but a failure in life. I have not succeeded in settling down. People take their normal lives for granted. But I . . . I have nothing by way of normal. Life has passed me by and left me only suffering'.

Gautam's voice was at once stern and compassionate: 'Stop feeling sorry for yourself. Don't own these labels, GP— these labels of being a failure, a success, normal and abnormal. These have no meaning at all in life.'

My misery and anger spiralled. Gautam was not getting it. He was simply not understanding what I was trying to impress upon him. My voice broke. 'Easy for you to say, Gautam. I am all of 33 years old, and I am struggling in every single area of life. My mother is gone. My father is 73, and I simply don't know how long he will be around. I don't want to be alone. I am lost. And my current situation is beyond miserable. The best years of my life have passed me by. Why can't you understand the enormity of this issue? This reality of my situation?'

The reality of your situation is not the impossibility of it. It is your perception that makes it impossible. Your life is your environment. Your environment is nothing but a reflection of your innermost self.

Gautam looked at me, and his voice rang with power and certainty: 'The reality of your situation is not the impossibility of it. It is your perception that makes it impossible. Your life is your environment. Your environment is nothing but a reflection of your innermost self. Change this way of thinking, GP. Change the story you are telling yourself. Once you do, you will change and when you change, your situation in life will as well.'

I wanted so desperately to believe him. I wanted to grasp the rope he was holding out and draw myself to the shores that beckoned. But the twin miseries of lost time and my regret at my wrong decisions rode me hard. My tears plopped softly in the tall glass before me, adding to the condensation that already enveloped the glass and making my hand even more clammy. It felt like an act of courage to even lift my head. And even more to ask Gautam, 'Really? Do you think it is possible to find happiness? Do you think I still have a shot at living and erasing the miseries of my life? A shot at somehow getting out of this mess of my life?'

Gautam's hands were clasping his glass in a gentle embrace. The look on his face and the expression in his eyes were nearly indescribable. Here was power, compassion and a wisdom that was beyond my experience. His magnificent voice enfolded me even as his words jolted me out of my misery: 'It is always possible to bring the mind to happiness, to experience hope, to uncover gratitude and appreciation. You must become the person who can create, sustain and nurture happiness. Relationships are just a part of it. Marriage and finding the right life partner are not the be-all and end-all.'

You must become the person who can create, sustain and nurture happiness. Relationships are just a part of it.

Gautam was now leaning forward. He continued, 'Not having a job or a partner and being single does not mean that you are broken, unemployable or unlovable. There is nothing out there that needs fixing except your understanding and your response to your circumstances.

'Life's events and your own response have kept you in a frenzy. A frenzy of fear and insecurity. Of anxiety. And in that frenzy, you have taken big decisions for bad reasons. So much of this frenzy stems from the fear inflicted by society. The fear of missing out in life. Society dictates the right age to marry. But tell me, GP, is there a right age to live? A right age to live well? A right age to start living life the way you are meant to—for your happiness, for you to bring happiness to those around you, to others who are suffering? Contentment with yourself and your life is a journey, and you need to start by taking the first steps on this journey.'

Even as I knew in my heart that what Gautam was saying was true, there was no easy acceptance within me. Oh, I knew that before I could hope for a better future, I needed to sort out the mess right here, right now. The legal mess, the mess of emotions and the mess that was my life. I was a victim, of such deep hurt that healing seemed impossible. I poured it all out. The sordid saga from start to finish. How was I going to deal with it all?

Gautam's next words shook me to my core: 'You need to do only three things to start your journey towards happiness. Just three things. And I am confident that you will do them very well indeed. The first is to start to bless CP and all those who have hurt you. I will go so far as to say that you must pray for their happiness. And the second . . .'

My scream of anguish stopped Gautam in his tracks. 'Pray for his happiness? Pray for the happiness of people who have threatened me and taken away my peace of mind? Bless the people who have said the most hurtful things about me, about my character and about my close friendships? My aunt and uncle sided with CP. My own brother, always in a tug of war with me over something or other, aided and abetted rumours about my character. I was helpless. I felt *so* helpless. There was no character certificate that I could produce to stop these vicious lies. There was no way out.

'You cannot be serious about this at all. I thought you were here to help me, not sabotage me even more.' The words rushed out, spewing from a well of helpless anger and deep wounds.

Gautam's voice was firm and compassionate. 'GP, you will not be able to move forward and out of this mess if you don't heed my advice. This situation, however messy and terrible, is the creation of your own inner state—your inability to make the right decisions, or live in a state of emotional balance, or trust life and, more importantly, to trust yourself to create a good life. All this blame that your brother and you have heaped on your father and your expectation that others will give you a good life are the causes of the misery you are experiencing now. You married for the wrong reasons. When the foundation, the genesis, of a decision is wrong, how will it yield good fruit? Marriage is not a way out of problems. As you have discovered for yourself, it can well create many more.

When the foundation, the genesis, of a decision is wrong, how will it yield good fruit? Marriage is not a way out of problems.

Ultimately, what others feel about us is based on their own limited perspective of life.

'Yes, I completely understand that attacks on your intent and character are hurtful and painful. But, ultimately, what others feel about us is based on their own limited perspective of life.

'If you continue down this road, your choices will keep dwindling, just like the hope you speak of. On the other hand, your future can be truly wonderful. All that you seek, you will be able to create, work towards and draw towards yourself.

'If, and only if, you are able to heal now. If and only if you stop drawing deep from the well of anger and rage within. If and only if you learn to create peace in your relationship with your father. If and only if you create peace in all your relationships. Your true blessings and prayers for CP's happiness are important not for him but to set you free. Your prayers and blessings for his happiness and the happiness of all those you consider your enemies are more about you and your happiness. Find your freedom. You need to stand up now and make a difference in your own life.'

Gautam's fierce conviction ripped away, for the moment, the dark fog of grief, pain and anxiety that loomed over my future. I spoke now with great care, afraid that the promise of a happier tomorrow could be as fragile as all my dreams and endeavours had been till now. I was fearful of hope itself. I finally asked, 'What do I need to do, and how should I go about it?'

By degrees, little by little, from moment to moment, a wise man removes his own impurities, as a smith removes the dross of silver.

—The Buddha (*The Dhammapada*)

GAUTAM'S GUIDANCE

Gautam's guidance to me had three elements, with several steps in each. The three priorities that he guided me towards that day were, first, to set myself free emotionally and to heal. The second was to actively work on regaining my physical health. The third was to work on finding employment.

Gautam explained that the act of blessing those who had deeply hurt me and actively worked to destroy my reputation was critical to starting the healing process and becoming emotionally free. It was the most crucial element of his guidance. The first step was to draw up a list of the names of each person who had played a negative role in my debacle, and then to send them wishes, thoughts and prayers for their happiness.

I knew that I could not be sincere about it. Would it be enough to just go through the motions of it all? Gautam surprised me by saying yes when I asked this question. 'Yes, GP, start by doing it mechanically. Start because I am telling you to do it. Start because I say to you that it is the only way to change your own future. Start because, without healing emotionally, you will invite disease and distress beyond your imagination into your life. So just do it.'

The next element was to create physical health and bring back a sense of well-being. For this, I was to consistently do three things. One was to choose a form of physical exercise for at least forty to fifty minutes a day. The second was to eat one self-cooked, nutritious meal. Anything that appealed.

Something simple and doable. And the third was to listen to music that I liked. Anything at all. Any genre that I could spend thirty minutes a day listening to.

I decided to kill two birds with one stone. I had a Sony Walkman that I'd bought for 10 dollars at a yard sale in the US. It was a sports model in a dashing yellow colour with not only a cassette player but AM and FM stations too. I could play a tape of my choice and walk with the music, fulfilling two of the conditions at the same time. And so I did.

Cooking one meal for myself was hardly difficult. I could cook for my father at the same time. My choices were eclectic and varied, from scrambled eggs to a simple dal or scrambled paneer. One day I made a kulfi from scratch and it was pretty awful, but my dad, with his weakness for all things sweet, relished it. I could not help but be amused by his enthusiasm.

With the help of some old cookbooks that belonged to my mother, I started putting together simple soups and tried to recall as much as I could of what my mother and my grandmother had taught me over the years. Just one meal a day.

The third and final element was to spend six hours a day making phone calls and poring over job advertisements. Six hours dedicated to finding employment and talking to people about finding employment. Letting even casual acquaintances know that I was looking for a job. Visiting consultants and placement firms that could help me in this quest. Those hours had to be utilized in this manner, irrespective of everything else. Irrespective of the time spent driving myself and commuting to an interview. Even on days when I had no will and no energy. Even as interview after interview was one of rejection.

The regimen was simple yet difficult to follow initially. But by and by, I fell into a rhythm that soothed my bruised emotions and my violated self-esteem. I started feeling more settled than ever for the first time since XLRI, which was a good eight years ago. There were small, defined steps to be taken each day without fail. There was work to be done, however humble. If I decided to try my hand at making a tomato soup, I also had to ensure that all the ingredients were available and the vegetables were well-washed and prepared.

Each call and attempt to look for employment made me interact with more people and learn to answer tough questions with greater poise. Yes, there was a gap on my resumé. Yes, I had not done well despite the MBA from XLRI. Yes, personal circumstances had hindered me in my professional life. Yes, I had come back from the United States with a master's degree left incomplete. Yes, this was my life.

I did keep quiet about the short-lived marriage and divorce. I knew it would not serve me well, both professionally and personally.

The effort involved in sending blessings, prayers and good wishes to the long list of those who had hurt and harmed me was immense. For weeks, I struggled and did it mechanically. And then it became easier to do so. I was more relaxed about it. Something so negative had unfolded in my life, but perhaps whatever I was doing now was ending it. Reversing it. Perhaps from the negative, I could build and craft something positive. It was time to end the negativity that had brought me to this sorry place.

There were possibilities in life yet to be explored. Perhaps it would all fall into place. I could live. I would live. Suddenly, there was a new hope.

BRICK BY BRICK AND DAY BY DAY

IN WHICH I RECLAIM MY LIFE

Right vision consists in knowledge concerning
Suffering, the cause of suffering, the cessation of suffering
And the path that leads to the cessation of suffering.

Right effort consists in exerting the mind so that evil and
unhealthy mental states do not arise, and that good and
healthy mental states do arise.

Right awareness consists in being aware of the body,
Sensations, thoughts and states of mind.

—The Buddha (*Maha Satipatthana Sutra*)

Even in the utter misery of those 33 years, I had learned one thing about life. One simply had to hold on to one belief, to one anchor or to repose one's trust in just one thing to make it through. Only one thing was enough. Just as one light is enough to banish the darkness. After all, when you board a bus, you place your faith in the bus driver to safely get you to where you need to go.

We don't really think about having faith in everyday matters. Yet so much of life is about having faith—in the chemist to give us the right and genuine medicines; in the doctor to diagnose and treat us correctly; in the government to do its work and somehow help us chug along in everyday life; in the organizations where we are employed to recognize us, treat us with respect and give us our salaries at the end of the month; in the staff we hire to help us with domestic chores.

I consciously decided to stop believing in astrologers and all those who were giving me conflicting views and advice. I consciously decided to believe in Gautam's words and to do as he asked me to do. With this decision, I had more time and more energy.

Gautam's advice was my one thing. The only thing I would follow. Having hit rock-bottom, I had pretty much nothing left to lose. I needed to accept his way with the hope that it would work out. It may well be the answer to my plight. I wouldn't know until I tried it out. I was fed up with trying the various remedies and mantras given to me by astrologers. I was fed up with my situation, my problems and my life. I was fed up with myself.

You may remember that the first guidance was to bless CP and all those who had hurt me beyond limits. I created a list and kept it by my bedside. I would feel choked and enraged just looking at the names—CP, his mother, a host of close relatives who were quick to accept the false narratives about me, and many others who had added fuel to the fire or just blamed me for whatever stories had been spun to discredit and shame me.

I began by very mechanically blessing all of them. It was one of the most difficult things I had ever done or would ever do. In my own way, I prayed for them to be happy. So, when would my life change? When would I experience the transformation that I had now begun to believe would happen? Where was the breakthrough that Gautam's conversation with me had led me to expect?

Slowly, bit by bit, I started to calm down. The hard nucleus of anger was softening within. I started to have better and calmer interactions with my father. I could hold back the bitter accusations and relentless blame that had earlier marked my every conversation with him and every thought about him. We started to have one meal a day together despite our very different schedules.

The daily walk with music was softening the edges of depression and desperation. There was an element of enjoyment in the physical exercise and the music that was liberating. The early hours of the morning settled me emotionally. That walk in the rising sun made me less frantic. It made the day ahead more palatable.

The planning and preparation of one meal a day took thought and practical action. It was a good distraction that worked to bring down my stress and anxiety. I started to get more and more creative with it and to enjoy the rhythm of looking up the recipes and putting the ingredients together. I had to step out of our apartment to go and buy whatever was needed from the local market. And since I did this three times a week, I really had to plan ahead and put my list together.

The discipline of six hours of effort towards a job opened my life and my mind. I was compelled to read the newspaper advertisements with attention. I knew I could not meet the six-hour target based on newspapers alone. I was forced to interact with more people and simply build the courage to ask for help.

And then many things fell into place. I finally got that most coveted and longed-for job offer from a boutique consulting firm. It was a humble salary, but the job was with a very respectable firm, and it was the answer to many prayers. It was within driving distance, which my ancient Maruti 800 could manage. Provided, of course, I didn't use the AC while driving. What the heck! I could do it. And perhaps I would soon save enough money to buy a new and better car.

The daily effort spent on one meal was nourishing my body and mind. My health had improved, and my father, too, was looking and feeling much better. He was still frail, but it seemed that he did not need all the medication that he had been on for the past twenty years or so.

The daily walk and its accompanying music had made me a few shades fitter and more energetic. I could meet the demands of the daily drive to Delhi, long working hours and the responsibility of looking after my father and the house without collapsing and even with a degree of enjoyment. As I worked longer and longer hours, my father stepped up and took on some of the household responsibilities, such as ordering groceries and attending to the maintenance of the apartment. This improved not just my life but also his mental and physical health. He was looking much better and fitter and taking an interest in everything around him and in my life as well. We were bonding better, with greater ease and cordiality. With my time freed up, I could use my weekend in a better way. I could go see a movie with a friend and occasionally with my dad. Sometimes I could take my dad out for a meal. I could go buy books and even browse crowded markets for a wardrobe makeover.

I went from strength to strength in my work. Within six months, I had an increment of over 50 per cent in my salary. It was still not a huge figure, but my gratitude made it abundant. I was just grateful. It was time to buy the new car, in addition to so much more. It was time to contribute financially and take care of my father. It was time to stand up. It was time to live.

There were days and moments when my prayers for those who had so deeply hurt me soared to the heavens. My prayers and blessings were now from my heart. I had understood that my freedom and my happiness lay in them.

After refusing to consider a divorce and letting me languish in a state where I was neither single nor married, CP had come around to seeking a divorce on mutual consent. Yes, it had taken two whole years, but it had worked out. The occasional court date, which inevitably meant a meeting with him, no longer sparked the twins of deep loathing and fear in me. It no longer set off the tremor in my legs, the dizziness in my head or the feeling of being sick in my tummy. I felt an equanimity within, and I was able to remind myself that I had nothing to fear from someone I was praying for and sending blessings towards.

I could see and feel the difference. I had a sense of accomplishment. And with the sense of accomplishment, I experienced a feeling of happiness and developed a much-needed sense of self-efficacy and self-worth. The realization that I could be in control of my own life helped me blossom. I was growing as a person, as a human being.

I could see not just the light at the end of the tunnel but the end of the tunnel itself. Soon, I would emerge into the light. There was both light and lightheartedness. This was something I had not experienced since my mother had passed away—in fact, since earlier. I sensed the next breakthrough was coming my way. Whatever its shape and dimension, I had something to look forward to. The future held out infinite hope. The future held great promise. I could work my way towards it. I would work my way towards it!

'Do not think lightly of good, saying, "It will not come to me." Even as a water pot is filled by the falling of drops, so the wise man, gathering it drop by drop, fills himself with good.'

—The Buddha (*The Dhammapada*)

A PRINCE CHOOSES ENLIGHTENMENT

The council headman, the *mukhiya*, was worried. He, Suddhodana, had vowed to keep his son on the desired career track of succession to the head of the council seat—the throne. He made sure those around the young boy and, later on, the young man protected his son from any of the signs of the prediction. He went to the extent of insulating a large part of the city from the ugly sights of illness, death and poverty.

As was the practice of the time, Siddhartha was given a good education, including complete martial training. Siddhartha was expected to be able to defend and attack in keeping with his station in life. This training was part of his duty to become a better ruler, take up the responsibility of protecting his land and his people, and expand his territory.

Descriptions abound of the prince's strength, energy and mastery of the various arts. As a young man, he was 'a handsome nobleman, capable of leading a crack army or a troop of elephants' (*Sutta Nipata*, the Collection of Discourses). Other accounts describe the prince as 'handsome' and 'pleasing to the eye'. And others still describe him as having a godlike form and countenance. Prince Siddhartha was perhaps 6 feet tall, with dark or black hair. He was undoubtedly strikingly handsome. Various reports exist of his strong and mellifluous voice.

Several accounts from historical and Buddhist texts reflect on the care lavished on the prince. Records speak of his fine garments, retinue of servants and several palaces. It is said that Suddhodana built three palaces for Siddhartha. These were respectively five, seven and nine storeys, one each for the prevailing three seasons.

Many accounts of his life portray an excessively affectionate and, dare I say it, controlling father. Suddhodana was no different from the vast majority of parents who seek to shape the destiny of their children by encouraging, planning for and even dictating the right course of education, career and even a life partner. After all, they have their child's best interests at heart. The belief is that they know best.

An early marriage was planned for Siddhartha. This would serve two ends—to keep him attached to worldly life and to honour tradition. Suddhodana identified a young girl, Yashodhara, as the right match for his son. Perhaps she was part of the extended family, making it that much easier to know her real nature and identify her as **the** right match.

When Yashodhara's father was asked for his daughter's hand in marriage, he answered that the young prince must first prove himself worthy of winning the hand of the beautiful young maiden. Yashodhara would be given in marriage only to someone who proved worthy of her hand.

The suitors had to win her hand by excelling in varied contests. Siddhartha is said to have defeated all the contestants and proved himself superior in various skills. It is said that he was first in contests of literature and numbers, as well as wrestling and archery. With Siddhartha having proved his worthiness, the marriage was celebrated after some time.

Among those defeated were Ananda and Devadutta, relatives of the young prince, perhaps cousins. They were to play crucial roles in the later life of the young prince. Ananda went on to become the foremost and closest disciple of the Buddha. He served the Buddha with great devotion and was his aide until the Buddha's death. Devadutta's defeat, on the other hand, sowed in him the seeds of anger, envy and jealousy against the prince Siddhartha. These dark seeds bloomed into terrifying violence and jealousy after Siddhartha's enlightenment. Devadutta became a lifelong enemy of the

Buddha, going so far as to conspire against him, ruin his reputation and repeatedly attempt to kill him.

The foresight of the soothsayers was not in vain, and one by one, their predictions started to come true. Siddhartha witnessed the four life-changing sights: that of an old man, that of an ill person, that of a dead body and that of a calm, peaceful ascetic. The young man was confronted with the frailty of the human body, the impermanence of youth and strength, and the inescapable finality of life ending in death, as well as the possibility of peace and contentment without the clutter of others' expectations, things and even relationships to confine the quest for finding the truth of life.

When these sightings were reported to Suddhodana, he surrounded the pleasure palace of the prince with triple walls and increased the number of guards. He commanded the court dancers and entertainers to exercise their skills and divert the prince's thoughts through music and pleasure. It did not appear to have the desired impact.

And so it was that Siddhartha asked for his father's permission to pursue a higher calling and leave home in his quest for an understanding of the true nature of life. Suddhodana asked Siddhartha to ask him for any boon, anything to stop him from leaving home.

Siddhartha asked his father to grant him four things: first, to remain ever young; second, to remain ever healthy; third, to be able to live forever or attain immortality; and finally, to never be subject to decay.

His father was overcome by grief when he heard these words, as the prince desired what could not be granted by anyone. Even as the father outwardly consented to the son's desire to leave home, the king could not. Suddhodana increased the controls and guards both within and outside the palace. It was clear that the king would not allow his son to leave even after this discussion.

Siddhartha moved out of the palace one full moon night in the month of *Asadha* of the Hindu calendar (June–July).

He wended his path to the forest, there to follow his inner calling and to explore the truth of life and freedom from life's suffering.

Modern and even ancient reactions to this departure from a princely life of comfort and ease greatly differ. Many people believe it was wonderful that a young prince could leave home in the pursuit of a higher calling and then go on to illuminate the world with his wisdom and compassion. Some scoff at his action as escapism and point out Siddharth's irresponsibility in leaving his wife and child. An abandonment, if you will. Only the wise understand that Siddhartha deeply considered and reflected on this departure, The Great Renunciation. His sense of responsibility was keen and sharp. After all, the character of the young prince formed the foundation of his future enlightenment.

Struggle is inherent in any quest, defining life itself. So, too, struggle was a part of Siddhartha's chosen path. He followed severe austerities over months and years. It is said that he was emaciated to the point of becoming a skeleton—a bag of skin and bones—after starving for days as part of the austere practices that were believed to lead to enlightenment. He would consume a single grain of rice or a single sesame seed in the course of a day and over several weeks.

His strong warrior's body dwindled. One day, he was overcome with severe pain, fainted and fell unconscious. When he revived, Siddhartha realized that starvation and subjecting the body to extreme conditions were not leading him to happiness, growth or enlightenment. He realized that the true way is not to be found by one who has lost his strength. He made the decision to move away from this extreme practice and began to accept food as alms.

At this critical juncture, his existing five disciples thought that Gautama had not been able to attain enlightenment even after six years of the most severe austerities and that he was even less likely to do so after having started to eat ordinary food. These five followers, or, as they are called, the Five Disciples, left the Buddha and went away. The Five Disciples included the soothsayer, Kondana, present at the time of Siddhartha's naming ceremony.

This rejection of extreme austerity and self-denial was to mark a turning point in Siddhartha's journey. Having been raised in plenty as a prince, he already knew the other extreme of self-indulgence was not the way to happiness. He had explored austerity to its limits. He now knew that self-torture and unnatural austerity were not the way to happiness either.

Balance, what came to be known as the Middle Path, was to become the hallmark of his teachings to come.

With this understanding that enlightenment would not come about through severe austerity, Siddhartha would continue with his quest. On a full moon day in the month of May (probably at the age of 35), Gautama resolved that the day would end with his having attained enlightenment. After bathing and wearing his robes, Gautama accepted a bowl of thin rice gruel, which a young girl called Sujata offered him.

Siddhartha's quest, as lore has it, ended under the Bodhi Tree in Gaya, where he attained enlightenment in a meditative state. He awakened to his own Buddha nature, his highest self. He understood the true meaning of life and all that it contained.

Seven weeks after awakening to this highest state of life, the Buddha returned again to the seat of his enlightenment. And there, doubts arose in his mind about whether it would be possible to make this path of enlightenment known to others. Further reflection (a plea from the gods, it is said) made him overcome his own natural hesitation to share his learning with others.

Having decided to share his enlightenment with others, the Buddha took quick action. He resolved to find his first five disciples and wended his way towards Varanasi. Upon spotting the Buddha in the distance, Kondana (the soothsayer and former disciple) said to the others, 'My friends, here comes Gautama. We owe him no reverence since he has returned to free use of the necessities of life and has recovered his strength and beauty. However, as he is well-born, we will prepare a seat for him.' But the presence of the Buddha was so benign and wonderful that, despite themselves, the five rose from their seats and bowed before him in all reverence.

And so, seven weeks after attaining enlightenment, the Buddha gave his first sermon, his first discourse and his first teaching. The Buddha taught his five disciples about the Middle Path—the path between a single-minded pursuit of pleasure and a devotion to mindless self-mortification. The Middle Path, he said, is the way to opening the eyes and understanding that leads to peace, insight and higher wisdom. This path has eight steps: Right View, Right Aspiration, Right Speech, Right Conduct, Right Livelihood, Right Effort, Right Mindfulness and Right Concentration.

The journey of the enlightened Gautama Buddha was not easy. And it was to continue over the next forty-six years of his life. For he lived to be 80.

'It is frightening to leave our old selves behind, because they are the only way we know how to live. Even if the familiar is unsatisfactory, we tend to cling to it because we are afraid of the unknown.'

—Karen Armstrong in *Buddha*

LOVE AND HEARTBREAK

'No one is going to love exactly like you imagine.
No one is ever going to read your mind and take
every star from the sky at the perfect time and
hand it to you. No one is going to show up at your
door on a horse, with a shoe you lost'

—Stephanie Bennet-Henry

I experienced togetherness again, perhaps touched by love. After all, I had yearned for it for so long and so deeply. But love—it left me more vulnerable, more needy and with a heartache that seemed endless.

But I must go back a couple of steps.

With my newfound happiness, the security of work and employment, the divorce behind me and a deepening friendship with my father, it seemed the sun was shining brightly on my life and all was well. My perspective had changed. So had my approach and attitude to life. This was something I had never thought would be possible. I was happy. More so, I was content. Healed. Proud of myself.

I was looking better than ever. All the physical activity and the regimen of daily walks had done me good. I was an independent woman in her prime. Much beyond my hopes was right in my life. Touchwood! Perhaps it was the result of unbounded prayers, persistence in doing the right things and the dogged pursuit of a full life.

Though life was interesting and there was hope for the future, a deep hunger lurked within me. The hunger for love, the hunger for deepened human contact and the hunger for intimacy. Not just physical intimacy but a desire for the sharing of life and its special moments in the present and the future. Something that would bring about the family I yearned for. Something that would make me feel complete and make life normal. Something that would take away the feelings of loneliness I experienced so often.

Driving back from work late in the evening was at once a pleasure and an experience of loneliness. I longed for companionship. Someone with whom to share my delight in the everyday and the miracle that had turned my life around. Someone who could share my thoughts and even my purpose. Someone with whom I could discuss stuff. Just everyday stuff.

The fact was that time was moving. Fast. My dad was old and not always in the best of health. The fear of becoming totally alone lurked close, circling like a great white around its prey. Besides, it would just be nice to have a normal life—a normal life partner, do normal stuff and just be normal. You get my drift! After all, so much that was abnormal had already happened. I wanted to, and *needed* to, feel normal about life and the past. I needed to somehow catch up with life and make up for the time and years lost to me. For the normalcy lost to me.

After a few regular meetings and interactions, my contact with Gautam had become sporadic at best. Perhaps I was shying away from hearing the real truth about my life. It was an uncomfortable exercise to look at my unvarnished truths. Beyond this discomfort, to continue to work on myself, I needed commitment and courage. I was pretty much okay with letting things be, content to drift and cruise for the time being.

Until Arjun stopped all calls. Until I felt my heart break one more time.

A mutual friend had made the fateful introduction to him. He had a deep baritone and enthralling words. His pursuit of me had been swift and clear. He claimed to have fallen in love with me from the get-go. There was an attraction. We both shared a love for literature and Scrabble. We both loved theatre. Our ability to communicate effortlessly was a shared talent.

Initially, I held firm to my refusal to get involved with a man who was struggling both personally and professionally. He was not legally free to be in a relationship. Arjun's divorce had become a long-drawn affair in the courts, stretching to an impossible nine years at the time of our meeting. His career was stumbling around on drunken legs. His credit-card debt was alarmingly real. He was simply not the kind of person I envisioned marrying. Simply not the kind of life partner I needed or desired. Having just broken free from the tentacles of multiple problems, I needed someone who did not need looking after or sorting out like a major life project. Yet, ironically enough, I found myself drawn to someone who *was* exactly that. And if I longed to be married, then marriage would continue to be denied to me with his divorce still pending. Date after court date remained circled in red on both our calendars.

For nearly a year, I thought I was clear that I would not get carried away in this relationship. I would steer clear of a commitment. It would just be a friendship and partnership of shared interests, with the added thrill of mutual attraction.

We had a few things and a few friends in common. It was good to have a man's company for dinners and even drives around town. His voice could charm the socks off any woman, and he knew exactly how to make me feel wanted, appreciated and even loved. He would talk to me intently for hours. On the phone and in person. Making love is more than sex. It is seduction. It is courtship. It is a kind of wooing that lures.

Here was someone who listened to me intently. Let me correct that. Here was a man who listened to me intently. Here was a man who paid attention to me. He was caring in a way that I had not experienced in a long, long time. I was working hard and travelling across the country for work. He made it a point to meet my late-night flights and drive me across Delhi to my home in the suburbs. He made it a point to drive me home after a late-night movie that we caught together. He made it a point to look out for me. He noted how well the new white shirt suited me. How sexy the early morning husk over my voice made me sound in the everyday ritual of the morning phone call.

I was succumbing to the charm and attention. Something else was brewing besides friendship. Even though I knew that many elements were not right, I felt almost helpless in this attraction and began considering not just a light flirtation in the moment but a long-term relationship and, possibly, marriage as and when the situation allowed it. I learned to not care for the tiny voice of doubt within that sent up warnings from time to time.

My dad disapproved of the relationship, and he made his disapproval abundantly clear. Perhaps it served to push me closer to Arjun. The rebellious child within was still alive and kicking! My dad and even friends around me tried to get me to meet other people for marriage. In the initial days, this was fine with me. As time passed and emotions took over, I coolly informed my father of my decision to be in a relationship with Arjun.

Here was an intensity that matched mine. Here was an openness that matched mine. Here was also someone who had seen the worst side of life, much like me. I looked for and found much in common. Here, perhaps, was compatibility. Here, perhaps, was completion and happiness.

Until a certain coldness crept in. Until he showed indifference. Until that enthralling baritone showed its bite. Until my calls went unanswered. Until I was ghosted. Until there was silence.

Until my dreams were scattered around my feet. Until my heart broke.

'Every pain, every hurt, every frustration you ever feel on account of another human being should be engraved on your heart. Never ever forget them. Then make sure you never, ever do the same to a single human being. We all want to grow and be happy and creative. But the point we most often miss, is that some people's mission in our life is to teach us how to become a better human being through their negative example of how not to be.

'They are as powerful a teacher of how not to be as the person who is the greatest example of how to be.'

—Josei Toda, Second President of the Soka Gakkai

THE HELL OF LONELINESS

OUT IN THE COLD

abandoned
adjective
left completely and no longer used or wanted

Life was now mechanical. Get up, get ready and get to work. Get back home. Get to bed somehow. Repeat. An endless loop. I had lost the strength to fight. My father's quiet concern somehow added to my anguish.

The debris of my desires swirled in and out of my thoughts, sucking my emotions into a never-ending whirlpool of regret and self-doubt and finally casting me ashore. Alone. Always alone. The two years of knowing and loving Arjun were lost time. Time that I could have used to set up a home and create a family. Perhaps the finest time that I had. My prime time. I had swiftly moved south of my mid-30s. Not only was the biological clock ticking, it had boomed loud and clear. Only to become as mute as my hopes.

Work had always been a pleasure, something I delighted in. Now it was a refuge. I plunged into it with more and more desperation. Driving my fancy new car brought me no pleasure. The drive home that was used for bonding over the phone with Arjun was now solitary and silent. The dials on the car radio sat as untouched and unmoved as his heart. I had pleaded with him. I had tried going over to meet him under some pretext or another. Tried to reignite even a spark where once a fire had blazed. But the embers lay dead in a pile of ash. Only a dull memory remained.

My future seemed shrouded in despair. It seemed there would be no positive outcomes in life after all. All that I had aspired for and worked towards was a sham. Perhaps a payback for my own actions exactly eleven years ago. A lifetime ago.

Loneliness was my only friend. Faithful. Always by my side. Inside me. Engulfing me. Oh, I knew a lot of people. Colleagues. Friends. Many acquaintances with warmth and not just superficial conversation. But I was discovering the difference between knowing a lot of people and connecting with them. Spotting all the couples around me only brought pain and despair. Loneliness released its venom bit by bit into each cell of my life and flooded me with pain.

Finding strength each morning to face the day was a heavy chore. With my family history of bipolar disorder and my own acceptance of the genetic pull towards depression, I could feel the powerful tug of the quicksand of despair and hopelessness. Giving in was, at times, an alluring possibility. Yet, the work I had done on myself and the distance I had travelled after meeting Gautam would not let me give up or give in.

I needed help. Unscrambling my thoughts and my contact list, I dropped a message to Gautam, imploring him to meet me as soon as he possibly could.

Later that evening, battling a sense of déjà vu, I found myself in front of Gautam in our old Tea Shoppe spot. I opted for a cup of hot masala chai this time, while Gautam stuck with the cold peach tea. My daily crying jags had left me with a painful throat and a throbbing headache, and I had a vague thought that a hot cup of tea would help me more than a cold drink of any kind. Its fragrance wasted on me, I dully sipped my steaming tea while pouring my heart out to Gautam.

The aura of calm composure never left Gautam. Truly, I had never come across someone who could listen to another with this depth of intent and open acceptance. No matter what I shared with Gautam, there was no judgement on me, my choices or my stupidities. My voice wobbled in the telling, but Gautam's calmness got through to me, and somehow I ended my story feeling stronger and calmer.

Gautam was quiet. His silence became a bit unnerving. 'Say something, Gautam. What should I do? I am shattered yet again by life. All the effort I had made, all the ground I had gained after your guidance the first time we met—everything has come to an end and left me with nothing to hold on to. Today I may be doing well professionally, but I have nothing left to hope for—no marriage, no children and no family. I feel so desperate.

'All around me, the world moves in twos—everyone is paired up, and almost all my friends are married and well settled. For a brief time, with Arjun, I felt life was normal. I was part of a couple. I had someone to do things with. I have lost two whole years, perhaps my best years, in this relationship. I feel so cheated at the end of it all.'

As Gautam leaned forward, I was struck by his sheer good looks and to-die-for dark eyes. His presence was captivating, with his deep, mellifluous voice taking the entire experience to a whole new level of charm and fascination. Why on earth, I wondered, had I been avoiding meeting him? Was it because deep within I felt that Gautam may not approve of my relationship with Arjun? What had kept me away from the one person whose advice and guidance I fully trusted? Someone whose guidance had brought me progress and happiness in life. Why had I chosen to avoid it—to avoid him?

Being stood up, ghosted, rejected and dumped, however you term it, is a terrific opportunity to learn and grow. Provided, of course, you don't wallow in it.

Gautam's 'GP' jolted me, and I dragged my wandering thoughts back. He continued, 'The ending of a relationship and what you are calling heartbreak are not only about mourning. It is about reflection and learning. Being stood up, ghosted, rejected and dumped, however you term it, is a terrific opportunity to learn and grow. Provided, of course, you don't wallow in it. It is okay for you to be alone, whether just now or for the rest of your life. Your problem is not just this break-up or that break-up.'

'What do you mean?' I was bristling with resentment at not being understood by the one person I had been counting on for a sympathetic response. 'I have lost time. Time that was so precious, right in my mid-30s, for settling down and starting a family. I invested myself in this relationship. Gautam, why don't you understand my agony over this loss? It's not just the end of a relationship; it's the end of my future. Of my hopes to settle down, start a family and lead a normal, happy life'.

Despite my near rude and heated rejoinder, Gautam maintained his calm demeanour as he said, 'Whether it was the previous set of problems or your current one of heartbreak and loneliness, they all stem from you not having spent enough time to get to know your own self. People only mirror our own relationship with ourselves.

People only mirror our own relationship with ourselves.

'Loneliness is not really about how many people you have in your life or the relationships around you. It is about how you feel about those people and those relationships. And loneliness is very much about how you feel about yourself and about your own life.

'You have to change your understanding of what matters in life. You have bought into the story of life moving a certain way, in a certain direction, with clear milestones at different times—study, qualify, work, get married and have children. All of this must be done by a due date or else . . . or else, what? Will it expire? Will the possibility of happiness in life expire?

'Yes, many people do live their lives in this way. And I hope that they understand that life is not about just being "normal" or crossing milestones when expected, but about being happy, content and excited while doing so.'

The conviction and clarity in Gautam's words and voice bowled me over for a moment. It took me a while to gather myself and choke out, 'I am so lonely, Gautam. So very lonely. I don't know how to handle this loneliness.'

> *Loneliness has to be understood and used. It has to be resolved. But not by rushing into another relationship. Not by killing yourself with emotional hurt. Not by working insane hours.*

'GP, loneliness has to be understood and used. It has to be resolved. But not by rushing into another relationship. Not by killing yourself with emotional hurt. Not by working insane hours. If you say Arjun was in the wrong, why are you hurting yourself? You could never have transformed his character or changed him. Arjun has, in a way, done you a great favour. Always remember that when a relationship ends, life is giving you a chance for a new experience.

> *Always remember that when a relationship ends, life is giving you a chance for a new experience.*

'Start by becoming the best of friends with yourself. You have been living in a state of reaction to everything and everyone around you for the longest time. Here is a brilliant timeout! Take five. Detox on an emotional plane. Let go of the emotional clutter within. Externally and professionally, so much has been sorted out—you are doing well. You have fought long and hard to create significant breakthroughs. You have begun to be thankful for the blessings in your life. Now begin the work of understanding yourself. Begin the work to be your own best friend.

'Even if, early tomorrow morning, you bump into the right guy, there is no guarantee that you will never experience loneliness again. Go beyond the notion that your soulmate is someone else. For all of us, we are our first soulmate. We are the one we are with when we take our last breath. Isn't it time to explore this one relationship? And as you do, I know that you will emerge strong and complete.

Go beyond the notion that your soulmate is someone else. For all of us, we are our first soulmate. We are the one we are with when we take our last breath. Isn't it time to explore this one relationship?

'Even people who have been married for the longest time, who are with their chosen mates and who have a loving family experience loneliness. You can still experience it, even in the midst of the most interesting party ever, surrounded by friends and even family.

'So, why don't you stop lamenting? Just this once, stop whining and moaning.'

Gautam's words stunned me out of my own misery. How would I do all this? How would I move forward? Where was my blueprint to find my way to myself?

'If you feel lonely in a relationship, fill that void through yourself. If you seek the solution to loneliness in other people, the cycle never ends.'

—Raga D'Silva (in a personal chat)

GAUTAM'S GUIDANCE

Gautam shared with me a clear way to stop suffering from loneliness. I was astonished at what he had to say. 'GP, the life of every single person, every single human being, is a solitary journey. We are all alone throughout our journey, from birth to death. The problem is that we don't enjoy our own company.

'This may have something to do with the fact that we don't really spend time getting to know ourselves except when we are truly young. If you stop and watch small children at play, they can be engaged for hours, just exploring, observing and talking to themselves. Even a discarded carton or an empty box is enough to keep them occupied. They are not experiencing loneliness, even though they are playing all alone.

'I say to you that being alone has to be enjoyed. Savoured. Relished. It is your opportunity to catch up with yourself. It is and can be a huge opportunity to achieve your goals, whether you aim to be fitter, more productive, more creative, more organized, healthier in body and mind, or calmer. Your time spent alone is about decluttering your emotions. If only you understand it and use it correctly, it is just the detox

Being alone has to be enjoyed. Savoured. Relished. It is your opportunity to catch up with yourself. It is and can be a huge opportunity to achieve your goals, whether you aim to be fitter, more productive, more creative, more organized, healthier in body and mind, or calmer. Your time spent alone is about decluttering your emotions.

you need to get more sorted in life and become mentally and emotionally stronger.

'All relationships need and demand time and investment to make them more enjoyable, more engaging and more rewarding. Relationships blossom when we make an effort to spend that time on them. This is equally true of your relationship with yourself.

'It all depends on how you are using the time alone—are you constantly browsing the net, are you compulsively shopping to fill the time, are you hooked on playing games on your phone, or perhaps binge watching?

'Or are you spending time caring for your body, your mind and your purpose? Are you talking to yourself and understanding what and who you want to be? Are you exploring what is important to you within yourself? Are you closer to gaining knowledge about who you are?

'We all know that every relationship has a vital role to play in our lives. Why, then, do we forget that our relationship with ourself also has a vital role to play in our life? This relationship needs care and commitment as much as any other. You can't grow older and then make time for yourself. If you don't learn to do it now, you will certainly not be able to enjoy this relationship decades from now.

'The Indian tradition of the four quadrants of life can be understood as a metaphor for leading a balanced life. It is not about spending twenty-five years studying, then setting up a home and family, and then detaching yourself from them. We can live the four states of *brahmacharya* (celibacy), *grihastha* (the householder's life), *vaan prastha* (withdrawal from society), and even *sanyaas* (renunciation) in the course of each day if we spend some time on gaining knowledge or skills, some time on nurturing relationships including the one with ourselves, and then enjoy our time out. And if you cannot do this every day, then make a plan that you can stick with to do so every alternate day or even thrice a week.

'Remember, *brahmacharya* is about complete focus on your work and on learning and skills that are important to you. It is about learning and being open to new experiences of life. *Grihastha* is about nurturing relationships around you and being nurtured by them. *Vaan prastha* is about self-care and focusing on yourself. Whenever you journal, reflect, meditate or workout by yourself, you are in the state of *vaan prastha*. *Sanyaas* is about becoming wiser and more understanding of life. It is about giving up whatever is unnecessary. Decluttering not just your space and your wardrobe but your life—physically, in your behaviour, in your approach and in your beliefs.

'I need you to do three things to overcome your loneliness. The first is to ensure that you spend twenty minutes each day with yourself. And before you rush in to say that you don't have twenty minutes each day, it could be every alternate day as well. Though I know that you can easily make time for these twenty minutes if you try.

'During this time, make sure that your mobile is nowhere near you and that nothing is pinging or bringing the outside world to you. Lock your door if you must. Keep a notepad and pen handy. Start to explore your own life bit by bit. Write what comes to mind. About your childhood, about your hopes for the future, and about yourself. About life. About your own hopes and your despair. About who you are. About who you would like to become as a person. How do you define progress for yourself?

How will you know you are progressing from day to day? What are the things you need to do to ensure that you are progressing?

'You can also simply start by thinking of these things, but my advice is to write. When we don't write and choose to sit and think, our thoughts are easily hijacked and start moving in one direction or another, like leaves gusting about in the wind. And so, writing helps much more. You can explore a new topic every day or stick to one theme for a week.

'Over a few months, you will start to understand who you are and what is important to you. Important only to you. Not because someone expects it of you. Not because someone says so. Not because that's how it's "supposed" to be.

'From this journal, get into the second habit of keeping another diary—your happiness and gratitude journal. Write in it each day. We all have things we can and must be grateful for and appreciative of. Without this spirit of appreciation and gratitude, we don't know and because we don't know, we don't understand how much is working well in our life. What all is working well and even why.

'Get a big, fat notebook that you love to look at and write in. Get one with good-quality paper and keep your best pen near it on your bedside table. Last thing at night, every night for the next 100 days, you will jot down three things that made you thankful or happy, that you are grateful for or appreciative of. From the smallest to the biggest. From what you dismiss as being insignificant to those that make you ecstatic. And watch yourself change over those 100 days!

'And finally, lose no opportunity to interact with people—friends, colleagues, strangers, anyone you come across. Talk to them about their lives.

Ask them how they are doing, and leave behind a small nugget of help or encouragement. The best way to overcome the painful sting of loneliness is by supporting, encouraging and helping others. Reach out to them with the intent of being an active listener. Share a bit of what you have learned and whatever has helped and encouraged you over the years.

'If someone invites you to a party or a get-together or asks you to attend a wedding, don't worry about going alone and standing out. Just go. If it means going beyond your comfort zone, so be it. Witness and observe the people around you. Enjoy even a brief interaction with a stranger.

'Just as every farmer knows that sowing is vital to reaping fruit or a crop, you must know that without sowing the right seeds in your life, you cannot expect the right results. I need you to become a farmer. Start sowing. Sow the seeds of expansion in your life and your inner self. Sow the seeds of friendship. Sow the seeds of knowing and loving yourself. Sow the seeds for being able to celebrate the ordinary, the normal, the usual and the everyday. With this, you can hope to bring your life to a rich harvest and reap its results.'

THE THREE MARKS (CHARACTERISTICS)

TRI LAKKANA

Impermanence (*sabbe sankhara annica*)
Unsatisfactoriness and its suffering (*sabbe sankhara dukkha*)
Insubstantiality (*sabbe dhamma annata*)

The philosophy of the Buddha precedes and captures in totality modern thought and confirms this one inescapable truth: it is a VUCA world. Volatility, uncertainty, complexity and ambiguity (VUCA) are all part of life. The Buddha was the first to consistently expound, for nearly fifty years, that life is volatile, uncertain and dynamic. Everything in life is in a state of flux and change. This is how life is. Period.

To ignore or reject, to sweep under the carpet this essential nature, this nature of life and the world, is unwise. Making decisions, taking action and responding to events through the filter of delusion creates baggage, leads to getting stuck and then creates frustration, disappointment and pain.

The common understanding of the Buddha's teachings as a philosophy of suffering is incomplete. The Buddha's entire endeavour was to help each person and humankind overcome the suffering of life, including bringing about the understanding that happiness is not permanent. Understanding and wholesomeness are less impermanent.

Think about a good physician who diagnoses and urges the patient to make lifestyle changes to live better and to prevent illness. The Buddha, too, diagnoses reasons for mental and emotional illnesses and suffering. With this clarity comes a prescription to live better and create conditions of health on the physical and more subtle planes of life.

What exactly is *dukkha*, or suffering? And what does it really have to do with relationships in life? And that too in the context of the world of the twenty-first century?

Suffering is anything that causes us to experience the pain of dissatisfaction, frustration or both. A less-than-satisfactory condition in life and relationships is suffering. And yet, in a world that is mostly less than satisfactory, such is the reality of life. Does this mean that we have to be resigned to the pain of this suffering? Or that we have to continue to suffer the VUCA elements of relationships, people and life?

The teaching of The Three Marks is all about that understanding of life that frees us from this suffering. To understand and accept the true nature of life is to stop suffering. From such acceptance and understanding, wisdom is born.

The teaching of The Three Marks is all about that understanding of life that frees us from this suffering. To understand and accept the true nature of life is to stop suffering. From such acceptance and understanding, wisdom is born.

Sometimes we have to undergo suffering in order to understand and accept life's truths. Sometimes we simply accept another's perspective and become wiser because of it. It helps us stop suffering.

And the source of wisdom can be as unexpected as a celebrity chat show! In his signature series of *Koffee with Karan* (Season 7, Episode 3), when Karan Johar says to his very glamorous guest who is experiencing the suffering of a 'failed relationship', 'when a relationship fails, it is not that you get a C. It is not a C, it is just life . . . Life takes over', he is actually taking a page from the Buddha's advice, and saying that such is life. Such is the nature of life and its relationships. A wise understanding of incomplete relationships and unsatisfactory conclusions. And one that gives hope for the future!

Overcoming suffering becomes possible through understanding. This quest to overcome suffering depends entirely on our own efforts. Making us the central figures in our own lives. Putting us in charge. Making the Buddha's teaching liberating and empowering.

The first characteristic of the nature of life is that nothing is permanent. The Pali *annica* is close to the Hindi *anishchay*—the undefined and even the ambiguous. Since nothing is defined or definitive in a life based on social conditioning, a life where trends and social and parental expectations dictate our life and the course of our actions, our work and effort cannot make us happy or lead us to a deeper fulfilment.

So, an acceptance of social diktats on what type of person we should marry, whom we ought to date, when we 'should settle down' and what their characteristics 'ought' to be is misleading or simply the wrong interpretation. Decisions, actions and responses largely based on people's opinions and social diktats are unlikely to lead to happiness.

Social expectations objectify people and relationships. Marry someone who looks good, is of a certain height, a certain weight, a prescribed shape, falls precisely into this desirable income bracket and comes from exactly this kind of social background. A person who is a bundle of characteristics rather than the person as a whole. In a world where characteristics keep changing—aka body weight, body shape, income and savings, health, and even sexual appetite and preferences—choosing a bundle of characteristics and expecting them to remain unchanged forever is setting the grounds for later dissatisfaction.

The second characteristic of life is the suffering inherent in it. Call it what you will—unhappiness, pain, dissatisfaction, disappointment or despair. This is the only problem that the world has. The Buddha said, 'The world is established on suffering' (*dukkhe loko patitthito*).

In the context of relationships, this characteristic has great meaning and significance. In the words of the Buddha, 'to be connected with what one dislikes is suffering; to be separated from what one likes is suffering'. Clinging to someone is suffering. Not getting what or even whom we desire is suffering. And not getting an outcome when we want one is also suffering.

Boredom is also suffering—a condition of dissatisfaction or unsatisfactoriness. Life in the twenty-first century seems to have enough and more of these—working with, living with and being related to those we dislike. Think about a difficult ex that someone is compelled to interact with and even share custody of a child or children with, a problematic in-law or many others. Interactions with those whom we truly dislike are the cause of suffering. And a separation from those we love, whether temporary or lasting, leads to pain. There is suffering in being jilted and ghosted. Suffering when a relationship comes to an end.

In his great wisdom, the Buddha knew and understood that suffering could be either physical or psychological. For those who are seeking love, the quest for love, clinging to the 'wrong' notions of it—romance and even marriage—or clinging to relationships of the past or clinging to the 'wrong' relationship itself causes pain. Not getting what we want and when we want it, cause us to suffer. Equally great is the suffering of unanswered expectations.

The right interpretation and understanding create conditions of calmness and composure. In the stillness of a calm mind arises deeper insight, or wisdom, if you will. With this wisdom, it is easier to make the right decisions and do the right things.

Choosing between staying in a relationship or leaving it? Base it on calm consideration. Choosing to marry? Base it on a deeper understanding of marriage, of life and of yourself. Of what is truly important to you—your priorities and your choices. As well as an understanding of the other person, their truth and the truth of the nature of life.

Choosing to enjoy a friendship with benefits? Know and understand that emotions can hijack casualness and that the end of the benefits can impact the friendship. Dealing with being ghosted? Accept that it happens. And know it is more about the other and less about you. Dealing with infidelity of some kind? Know that the right person can make a huge mistake, and also know that people repeat their patterns, showing us their true self. And so, we choose to act, to react, to respond and to decide in a way that reduces or stops our suffering—in the long term. This is happiness.

The third characteristic of non-self refers to the unsubstantiality of life and people. Possession of people and relationships isn't quite real. The philosopher Khalil Gibran expressed this so poignantly in these lines: 'They (your children) are the sons and daughters of life's longing for itself. They come through you but not from you, And though they are with you, yet they belong not to you'.

We enter into relationships and create labels, not accepting or knowing that both of us, as all of us, are a collection of changing characteristics and attributes. We are changing and hopefully evolving! As is the other person. Because we are changing and so is the other, a desire to stop our change or to hold on to the person who was a certain way when we started this particular relationship and this journey is futile. The more we expect this change to stop, the less happy we will become. Or the more we expect the other person to change, the greater unhappiness we experience. **The person simply is.** Their being a certain way may bring us great pleasure at one time, and then their being another way may cause us equally great unhappiness.

Impermanence in relationships, in people and in the world is not a cause for sorrow. Or anxiety. It is an opportunity for a positive change.

Impermanence in relationships, in people and in the world is not a cause for sorrow. Or anxiety. It is an opportunity for a positive change.

In a romantic relationship, in courtship and in marriage, the expectation that our partner will do or be exactly as we expect them to do or be, is certain to bring us suffering and pain. It is not the expectation that is a problem, but the insistence that our expectation is the only way. And must unfold exactly how and when we need it to or expect it to. Life is complex and subtle . . . we become happy when we understand that and hold our expectations gently and calmly.

Happiness in relationships is ours when we see and even create ways to transform situations and aspects of relationships from negative to positive. When we respond to people, to situations and to ourselves in ways to reduce suffering. When we interpret life and our relationships with kindness and positivity. When we use loving kindness as a technique in meditation, in our viewpoint and approach in everyday life **and** in every relationship.

> 'Neither mother nor father nor any other relative can do a man such good as is wrought by a rightly-directed mind.'
> —The Buddha (*The Dhammapada*)

STEP BY STEP

LEARNING TO LOVE, LEARNING TO LIVE

'No one is going to love exactly like you imagine.
No one is ever going to read your mind and take
every star from the sky at the perfect time and
hand it to you. No one is going to show up at your
door on a horse, with a shoe you lost.

**Do you understand? That's why you have to love
Yourself enough, so that any other love just adds
More candles to the cake you've already iced'**

—Stephanie Bennet-Henry

The party was on!

The invitations were sent out well in advance. I had always been knowledgeable and even passionate about food. My work with one of the world's finest hotel chains had only taken my understanding and love for food to another level. That night, I had the meal catered by a neighbour, with a few snacks made by my now-well-trained cook.

My dad also quite enjoyed himself, spending the first hour with the people milling around and then turning in for the night. In his heyday, he was an excellent host. My parents hosted parties with style and elan.

The night had become possible only because of the hard work I had put in, day after day, on myself. After the last meeting with Gautam, I spent many a night tossing and turning. It was not the despair of passing time and heartbreak that had given me sleepless nights. Rather, Gautam's words ricocheted like bullets inside my head. There was a deep truth in those words.

61

The application of Gautam's guidance was no easy task. It took hard work and discipline. Of time, of focus and even of my emotions. But I was beginning to see the results. An ease and a sense of contentment brewed in me. The distress was fading. I had somehow skirted the lip of the whirlpool and managed to not drown in it. I was working hard at my job, bringing my best self. At the same time, I was trying to create value in each aspect of my life. Once again, I was learning to enjoy life. And marriage was no longer central to my happiness.

Oh sure, I sought marriage still—for companionship, family and friendship. But not from a sense of being diminished without it. It was no longer driving each day and each interaction of my life. It would happen when it did. I was comfortable with myself and my life. The desperation that had driven me for the better part of my life was no longer in the driver's seat.

It was important to me to live a full life. To treat myself and others with respect. To resolve my problems and issues with all the resources I could gather—the advice of my father and a small handful of good friends, my own thoughts and books. My writing became my friend and my journal, a close companion. And of course, Gautam's advice, which always gave me a higher and different perspective. It was important to work hard. It was important to look after my father and myself. To make my home more comfortable. To grow. To enjoy that growth.

However, now was party time! There was nothing I enjoyed more than putting a party or an event together. There was a pleasant buzz to drawing up a list, making calls and putting together meaningful messages as invites and reminders. I enjoyed sprucing up the living room and putting out the fine china and the good flatware, my inheritance from my parents. I laid out crisp new towels in the kitchen and the washrooms. Animesh, the young florist at the corner of the road close to my apartment, was happy to deliver loose bundles of seasonal flowers that I placed in vases scattered around. Yes, it was not the last word in luxury or space. But it was mine, and I had learned not to wait for life to be perfect before I began living it.

Get-togethers at home also heralded a moment of deep regret that my parents' venerable record player and the large speakers that boasted the Ahujasons' label were no more. No more was my father's pride, his elaborate vinyl collection— the small records and large LPs, the awkwardly sized 78 rpms, aka the medium records, all lovingly placed in huge plastic sleeved albums. Ah! A moment of silence to mourn their loss! The fabulous collection housed LPs of James Last, the ebullient Andy Williams with his House of Bamboo, and Hindi film music, starting with the venerable K.L. Saigal to the more modern cha-cha to the soaring and versatile Asha Bhonsle and early R.D. Burman.

I made up for the loss with CDs that I played in a newly bought CD player, with the volume adjusted to a pleasing, discreet level.

Guests always seem to arrive in spurts, don't they? The first few trickle in, and then a few more arrive almost all together. Finally come the laggards, who almost take pride in the lateness of it all. Perhaps the pride stems from a very full calendar or a very full social life. To my elation, Gautam had agreed to drop in for a bit as well. He was almost never late, so I had asked him to arrive at a later time than that of the other invitees. I wanted my friends to meet him as much as I wanted him to see how well I was doing because of his advice and guidance.

Soon the snug living area had filled up. Friends had made themselves comfortable all across the not-too-large living room. They were on the sofa and deep chairs; some surrounded the dining area, from where they refused to let the snack platters move. A few were out on the tiny, plant-filled balcony. There was Superna, Aparna with her fiancée

Harsh, Reema with her husband Vikram, my friend Rajeev Churamani, who had dropped in for a bit, Shachi, Chirag, Prashant, Puneeta, Sudip . . .

I could see the interest and curiosity in my friends vis-à-vis Gautam, who stood out even in his white T-shirt and sky-blue denims combined with comfortable sandals. Of course, they all knew about this charming and somewhat mysterious man who had so wonderfully influenced the course of my life and brought me out of the mess that I had created. And somehow, all were gravitating towards Gautam in just a while.

As the night progressed the conversations became deeper, and then Superna, who had been struggling for the longest time with the pain of her singlehood, said, 'Gautam, it appears to me that I have truly failed in life. I need to get married, and it is the one thing that seems to elude me no matter what I do. I have been praying about it. I sincerely follow all the advice that astrologers give me. I try to meet as many people as I can, yet it seems that people keep rejecting me. I feel very unlucky in life. Perhaps it is the lack of money or status? Or maybe I am not enough in some way? I just don't know what to do.'

Was it just me, or did everyone around me seem arrested by Gautam's voice and his calm answer? 'Superna, with this state of mind and such a view of your own life, it is better if you don't attract anyone just yet. Low self-esteem and neediness are poor reasons for marriage. They cannot help you make the right decision.

> *Low self-esteem and neediness are poor reasons for marriage. They cannot help you make the right decision.*

'Do you know that we invariably attract people—friends and partners—who mirror our beliefs and values? We attract people on a similar plane of emotional wellbeing or emotional disturbance. Imagine attracting to yourself someone who has an equally sad perspective. First, you have to build yourself. Build your own muscle. You will need to really strengthen your life and your mind before you can hope to be the kind of person who can nurture and tend to a relationship. You must first tend to and nurture yourself. Besides, poor self-esteem and neediness just lower your attractiveness quotient.'

Superna's tears flowed copiously down her cheeks by the end of his speech. Hands reached out to give her the paper napkins I had so painstakingly arranged on the dining table. I did a silent eye roll and wondered if I had been as painful and maudlin in my misery six years ago. 'What do you mean, Gautam? What is wrong with me?'

If Gautam sighed at what must have felt like an action replay, it was certainly subtle. His reply was patient. 'You may perhaps like to ask yourself why you believe that marriage is the solution to your problems. It rarely is. It may well mark the start of many more problems. All of us enter marriage or a relationship with the hope that it will bring us happiness. And continue to postpone living a full life till that marriage happens. If such is the case, you need to snap out of this endless postponement of your life.

Expecting anyone else to fix your life sets you up for failure. You have to be happy with who you are before you enter a relationship.

'All the astrological advice in the world will not lead you to a happy marriage. In a sense, you don't really have to work towards getting married. When you continue to evolve as a person, someone finds you.

'The questions to ask yourself are: Am I the kind of person I like to be with? Do I enjoy my own thoughts? Do I enjoy my own company? Am I content being me? Am I creating a self and a life that will be wonderful for someone to share with me? Expecting anyone else to fix your life sets you up for failure.

You have to be happy with who you are before you enter a relationship.

'Yes, this takes great effort. Put effort into yourself, and then some effort goes into the universe with the intent to marry. You have to be open to the opportunity to meet people. You have to keep moving. Keep growing. If you stop, you block the process.

Let us say you get married tomorrow based on all that astrological advice. Can you honestly say you are prepared for marriage? Prayers are not about wishful thinking or daydreaming. A prayer is a resolve, a determination to work on oneself until that prayer is realized. Prayers are a means of preparing ourselves and our lives. A reminder to self, if you will.

'Superna, it takes great skill to be happy in life. And greater skill yet to be happy in adult relationships, to be happy in marriage. Each relationship in our lives is hard work. Good relationships are not effortless. Just as being fit and in good health depends on our effort, being happy depends on our conscious work on ourselves. It is a matter of effort. Of training ourselves. If you don't have a good relationship with yourself, how will you have a great relationship with someone else?'

Superna's voice was a shade steadier and a whole lot quieter when she asked, 'But why am I so unlucky in love? Everyone else around me finds it, and people in my circle and my age are getting married without all this training and effort that you speak of.'

Reema piped up, 'I don't know why you believe that it is effortless, Superna. I don't know if I ever shared with you that Mummy was so very worried for my marriage. It was simply not happening. That, too, despite the fact that I was doing so well professionally, working with one of the best multinationals and all that. And since you mentioned astrologers, let me tell you something. All the astrologers that Mummy consulted for my marriage said that there was no chance of marriage as per my horoscope. Not just one, but one after another.'

We were all riveted. It was odd hearing about astrology from the modern and self-reliant Reema. She was very grounded in her approach and attitude towards life and its issues. I often turned to her for practical advice. She had been helpful and supportive through my various problems. Gautam turned to Reema and gently asked the question uppermost in all our minds: 'So what did you do about it, Reema? Clearly, not only are you married, but we can see the affection and bond between Vikram and you.'

Reema spoke slowly: 'I think I was happy in my everyday life. Just like GP is living with her dad, I too was living with Mummy, having lost my father when I was much younger. My elder sister got married long ago and had her own struggles. She doesn't even live here in Delhi. I knew my mother was worried that I wasn't married yet, and it was really important to her that I settle down soon. I, too, felt the need for marriage. So much of that need came from peer pressure and the pressure of wanting to ease my mother's worry. But I explained to her and to myself that being happy was more important. With or without marriage. Doing well as a person is more important. And there is no time limit on getting married. It is okay if it takes time. It is more important to find the right person. It is more important to live well. And it is okay to get married late'.

I was struck by the similarity between my new approach and Reema's. I had now accepted that marriage is not a solution to existing family problems nor is it an escape from the present. My new perspective and Reema's had strength and flexibility. We were open to the possibilities of life without getting trapped in neediness. I silently applauded Reema's approach and her clarity.

I slowly interjected, 'I have been there, Superna. I also know very well about the fear that rises from singlehood. So much of that fear comes from social norms—fear of being single, fear of being too old, fear of being judged, and fear of being talked about. It is truly FOMO—the fear of missing out.'

Sudip Sehgal then pitched in. He had been an intent listener throughout. There was a calm understanding and acceptance in his words: 'I am still alone at 46. I have keenly felt the absence of a companion. A void. I think society doesn't take single people seriously. I **know** my parents and the extended family have not taken me seriously because I am not married. People don't respect me as much. I feel I get left out of family and friends' functions.'

Aparna had been listening intently to this interplay. Her left hand cradled her glass as intimately as her right cradled Harsh's. Their comfort with each other—the intimacy—was subtle but unmistakable. She said, somewhat hesitantly, 'Sometimes the delay is caused by someone's inability to get over the past. Maybe because of a rejection or even being ghosted. I couldn't move forward at one time because I had been in a relationship with someone for a long time. My emotional bond and attachment to him kept me single for a long time. I kept rejecting perfectly good guys. And this guy was simply not open to getting married, despite our sustained relationship. I kept thinking that it would change for the better. Somehow. Anytime now. But of course it didn't, and I had to make a very tough decision.'

The chatter had long ceased. Conversations had stopped. The continuing dialogue around Gautam was being heard intently by all. The spillover from the snug terrace back to the living room had gone unnoticed. Snacks were neglected, though there were thoughtful sips of drinks and a few discreetly used cigarettes.

Superna was clearly fascinated as others opened up about their lives and struggles. Her voice was more composed as she asked hesitantly, 'So how did you get out of the relationship, Aparna? What did you do?'

Aparna's voice carried a new note of firmness: 'I decided to be clear about my own priorities in life. Marriage is important to me. I wanted to be with someone who could commit to me wholly and not hold back or hold out. This aspect of compatibility is critical, isn't it?'

> 'Even though I didn't face any pressure for marriage from my family or my parents, society and my circle pressurized me, asking me when are you going to get married. I had decided I will get married when I know it is right for me and the person is right for me, however much time it takes. I am someone who has always followed my heart and my passion whether it is my work or personal life.'
>
> —Shibani Kashyap (in a personal chat)

Gautam was smiling at Aparna. 'Yes,' he said. 'I'm so delighted to hear about your experience in life, Aparna. Thank you for sharing something that many would have withheld. This amazing clarity is what is needed in life. What is acceptable and what simply isn't. And yet, it would have been so hard to do this. Taking that one step out and away from love and the invested time, emotion and hope for a future together.

'When someone experiences rejection or is left feeling used or duped in a long-term relationship, they end up blaming themselves even more. Self-blame, regret and self-recrimination are natural, but when they linger and colour all perspectives on life and love, that is when problems start. Don't let this deadlock you in any way. Yes, there is a world of hurt. But healing is possible. Getting over our regrets is possible and doable. The first step is to live without bitterness, for only then can we taste the sweetness of our experiences and of life.'

In the wee hours of the morning, as I set about the solitary and somehow soothing task of cleaning and sorting the living and dining areas, Gautam's words were as strong a presence in my home as the lingering aromas of perfume and smoke. The evening would stay with me for a long time. I was not alone in my life experiences and would never be. Perhaps love would find me at the right time. And that was fine. There was life and hope beyond that. For now, I was content and felt complete within.

'If, as one fares, one does not find a companion who is better or equal, let one resolutely pursue the solitary course; there can be no fellowship with the fool.'

—The Buddha (*The Dhammapada*)

... AND YET!

A RESTLESS PASSAGE OF TIME

'All I am saying is, don't equate your worth
to some archaic idea of what the best means . . .

. . . because you shouldn't have to have a special
someone in your life to feel included. In fact, the
most special someone in your life is you!'

—*Do Revenge*, the movie

I was content. And yet, I wasn't. Restlessness engulfed me.

Around that time, my close friend Tulika enrolled me in India's leading marriage portal. She convinced me to let her co-manage my account. At first, I was hesitant to give anyone this latitude. After all, I wasn't targeting the usual parental selection of a life partner. This wasn't about an arranged marriage. But my life was full between all that I juggled, and I could use her as a sounding board. I trusted her with my dreams and aspirations. After some time and a whole lot of reflection, I agreed that this was a good arrangement.

I did sift through profiles myself, too. The whole portal was set out with ease of use in mind. At one end of the spectrum were probably parents who used the portal to find suitable matches for their children. Many may have found it difficult or complicated had the site not been laid out to ease navigation. On the other end were a host of digital natives—young people who sought partners for meaningful relationships.

But ah . . . the fidgets, the whiffs of restlessness within. Why? Was it the lack of physical and emotional intimacy? Was it the annoying wait for algorithms and AI to trawl through data bytes and throw up the right person for me? Was it that it seemed there were no good guys to meet at work or even elsewhere?

Tulika's profile selection was sporadic. No, let me change that just a bit. She was perhaps more choosy than sporadic. Yes, she was throwing up the occasional profile and leaving extraordinary editorial comments in my mailbox—comments on looks, on how cunning, smart or sincere the guy seemed, on what was right or almost right about him.

Arreee . . . Shaadi mujhe karni hai, why all the editorial commentary? Leave it to me to gauge and understand them. I wanted to tell her that my intuition is pretty good.

I was no longer that weak-spined sissy, ready to cave in and do anything for love, including marry the wrong guy. I'd been there and done that, after all, I mused darkly. It was interesting that this newfound spine, this inner strength, gave me stunning clarity on what or, rather, who was wrong for me. Like Salman Khan, I wasn't afraid to mouth off, '*Ek baar commitment kar di . . .*' I wanted and was resolved to be wary and wise before that commitment.

> 'It is a difficult question. How to identify the right person? Of course, it has to be someone with similar values. Someone with similar priorities. But how will you know that until you are not clear on your values and priorities first. Knowing yourself is the first step.'
>
> —Padma Shri Dr Bibek Debroy (in a personal chat)

There was this 27-year-old who wrote passionately to the 38-year-old me. The impassioned note made for an interesting and even amusing read. But commitment?

Then there was the 40-something who spoke in circles. My dad really liked his email to me, for god's sake! Dad was convinced that this guy was very keen to marry me. The problem, of course, was that I was not keen at all to marry him. I felt no attraction to him in any way.

I was clear. Marriage would no longer be a compromise. It was no longer about what the world would like me to have, do or be. This was about me. Not in a loud, jarring, selfish way but in a quiet, gentle acceptance that I was important in the scheme of life.

And why not? The commitment was to me and not to the world or my dad. I had to live it and love it. It would be a commitment for life. Was I overthinking the matter? But it was necessary to be clear if I had to succeed in this vital relationship. My track record hadn't been the best. I had loved too deeply and ruined it all. I had tried being in a relationship without a happy ending. Was I simply jinxed? Why was love so elusive? Or, scratch that, why was lasting love so elusive?

I believed I was doing so much right. Making such a wonderful and conscious effort to live life well. And yet, there was no visible result. Month after month went by. And there was a growing restlessness. From restlessness, I was fast moving to a space of self-doubt with big dollops of sadness. I needed a new way of looking ahead and dealing with my past and the regrets that poked through the layers of time, effort and gratitude. I did try hard to break out of the emotional web. Dad, friends, books, movies, travel for work and solo vacations—a whole world of work and engagements. A spanking-new, big car. A comfortable life. No EMIs. A life of many blessings. A full life. But the restlessness simmered quietly. Gautam always said that the absence of something is always greater than the presence of many other things. Not the wisest way to be. Yet my reality . . .

I knew I needed help. I needed a new way of looking at things. Perhaps even a new set of beliefs and approaches. And I knew who could help me—Gautam.

We had entered another spring. There was a beauty, a crisp newness, to the air we were breathing. Gautam and I met in the sprawling grounds of the Lodi Gardens, the sky an endless blue and the sun warm and mellow that February morning. Gautam's elegance was timeless. He was in his invariable combination of comfort and pastels. This time, though, he had donned a handspun cotton kurta in the palest shade of peach, which he carried with his usual style and élan.

There is something special about spring and its blooms. The greens look more alive and greener than ever, there is a resurgence of hope within and a fresh energy moves through the world. Birds, animals, humans and the world of flora are all more lively, all a bit more infused with life.

I had to sift through a medley of thoughts and emotions and get to the point even as we hit our stride. I had to work hard at keeping up with Gautam's longer stride and not sound out of breath while talking.

As we paced ourselves, I told Gautam about this strange combination of restlessness and the strength I felt within. Gautam heard me with his characteristic calmness. He said, 'I am so glad that you are understanding and accepting your strengths and even your restlessness, GP. It takes courage to say no to what is wrong for you and to what does not work for you, and I know you have earned it the hard way. It is easy to say yes and get on with the relationship. It's easier to keep going with the flow and end up married. Because we all want celebration. And the courtship and all that leads to marriage as an act are the high points of that celebratory phase.'

It's easier to keep going with the flow and end up married. Because we all want celebration. And the courtship and all that leads to marriage as an act are the high points of that celebratory phase.

Birdsong was the pleasant warble underscoring Gautam's words. The voices of fellow walkers and others around us had somehow faded into the background.

I mulled over what he had said. I ventured somewhat tentatively, 'You mean that folks sometimes go with the flow or make the wrong choice just to go through the celebratory phase of it all?'

'Yes,' said Gautam. 'If you look back on your life, haven't some of your decisions been prompted by something similar? And why should you be the exception? Others find it easy to go along with the flow too—of the relationship, of the moment, of the expectations of their family. It is much easier to go with the flow than to resist it. Even when your gut is asking you to pause. Even if that little voice inside is telling you that it may not be quite right.'

'Gautam, is the solution a prolonged courtship? And how trustworthy is the feeling that a certain person is right for me? After all, people do get divorced after a prolonged relationship, courtship or even a long engagement. Things do go awry. So, is knowing someone for a long time any guarantee?'

I couldn't really see Gautam's face except in profile. But the smile was evident in his voice as he said, 'The problem lies in thinking that there is only one right person in the universe for you. There are several people who may be right for you.

'The ease of friendship is usually a good sign. You can evolve a relationship from friends to lovers and then to partners. Of course, for ease of mind and to savour relationships, be in one relationship at any time. Multiple relationships at the same time impose a strain on those in them. And even if they do not impose a strain, they stunt the growth of the people concerned. The purpose of all relationships is our growth as human beings.'

The purpose of all relationships is our growth as human beings.

'The purpose of all relationships is our growth as human beings.'

The words seemed to reverberate through me. My steps had slowed because suddenly Gautam was further away.

I moved fast to catch up, the words echoing in my mind. Somewhat out of breath, I asked, 'Do you really mean that? That the purpose of all relationships is our growth as human beings? Is that true of marriage'?

Gautam had set a brisk pace and moved swiftly. His breath was even, not winded like mine. So, his answer was steady and calm as ever: 'Of course, GP. The purpose of **all** relationships is our growth. When we enter into romantic relationships, when we partner with someone, and when we marry, it is about growing. Sometimes it is about growing because of the other person, sometimes growing with each other, and sometimes growing despite the other person.

When we enter into romantic relationships, when we partner with someone, and when we marry, it is about growing. Sometimes it is about growing because of the other person, sometimes growing with each other, and sometimes growing despite the other person.

'When there are similar strengths or something that complements ours, we grow together. When we learn from the other person—their behaviour, their weaknesses, their words, their stupidities and their wisdom—we are growing because of them. And when the other person turns away, is indifferent or there is a lack of friendship, we can still choose to grow despite the other.

'Enjoy yourself, of course. Enjoy and relish the romance and courtship. Enjoy the physical and mental companionship. Relish the intimate moments. But know that the purpose is to use that energy to grow. Become more—wiser, kinder, larger-hearted, better, more organized, more relaxed, more energized. Even more resourceful and more focused.'

Hmm. This was food for thought. A different way to look at love, romance and the whole brouhaha of it all. But how best to deal with my search and the restlessness I was experiencing?

Perhaps my voice carried my impatience as I voiced this thought: 'All this is fine, Gautam. But what am I to do about my uneasiness and impatience? I have done almost all the things you have asked me to. I know I am in a better space. I know I have become a better person in almost every way. But the jinx is still alive. How do I break out of it? How do I deal with the regret I experience when I look back in time?'

Gautam was patience itself, 'Which part of life is causing this regret? What is it about?'

I answered slowly, 'My biggest regret is the time I have wasted in various relationships. They didn't fructify in the way I expected; for instance, my most recent involvement with Arjun. It stands out for the regret it generates. I just feel so helpless and sad. Yet, no amount of regret over my decisions in the past and the way life unfolded helps me. I don't know why I am so jinxed in the matter of love.'

Gautam's answer hit me dead centre, leaving me stunned for the next few minutes. He said, 'GP, you have to understand one thing and one thing only. Every element of life is about your growth. Regrets are powerful in the lessons they teach us. Each relationship you had was a form of training. It worked to bring you a step closer to what you sought. Each relationship was training for life. Training for how to be in relationships. Training equally for how not to be. Each one uncovered for you the one aspect that you sought and that was right for you. If you are so sure today that you know what is right and what is wrong—what works for you and what does not—it is because of your lived experiences. Each relationship from the past is a matter

> *Regrets are powerful in the lessons they teach us. Each relationship you had was a form of training. It worked to bring you a step closer to what you sought. Each relationship was training for life. Training for how to be in relationships. Training equally for how not to be.*

of quiet gratitude and understanding. Not a matter of regret and pain.'

I don't know how long we walked in silence. The tall man walking by my side was a friend beyond compare. Truly my philosopher and guide. Gautam's words seeped in. This was a new way of understanding my past relationships. Here was a new way to free myself from regret and stop the disappointment.

> *Having that life partner is neither a guarantee of happiness nor a matter of completion. You can be happy, complete and fulfilled without a partner. You complete yourself. Period.*

More questions bubbled in my mind: 'So should I even be looking at getting married? I mean, is it okay to keep looking for a partner—a life partner? Or are my lessons over? What should I do at this juncture of life?'

'GP, the decision to marry or not is up to each individual. It is not a matter of destiny but of choice. Each person must be allowed to make the decision of whether or not they want to marry, how many children they want or not, and who they want to marry.

'Of course, it is fine to seek out a life partner, albeit in the full knowledge and acceptance that getting or having that life partner is neither a guarantee of happiness nor a matter of completion. You can be happy, complete and fulfilled without a partner. You complete yourself. Period.

You must work to become happy, complete and fulfilled. And if someone falls in step with you and shares your life, it is an option that you choose to exercise. It is a choice that should be made in the right frame of mind and with the right set of emotions. Or, let me put it another way—marry for the right reasons only.

'Ultimately, the more coherent your reasons, the better your understanding of it all, the wiser and better your choices—whether in life, in accepting companionship, or in your choice of a partner. And the better your ability to nurture all relationships. Including the one with yourself.

'Partnerships and marriage transform men and women if you allow them to. They are not about one person imposing their will or their diktat on the other or insisting you become a certain way. It is about what you allow and what you choose to become in the course of the relationship. And how you choose to contribute to the world at large. A relationship, intimacy, partnership, marriage—all these are about meaningful shifts in life and in consciousness. Relationships are about how you choose to relate to one another; they're about growing.'

'But why is it taking so long for me? When am I likely to find the right person?'

'GP, it is what I just said. The world thinks only in terms of one person being the right one. One soulmate. But it is a universe of possibilities. You, just as anyone else, will meet a number of people who fit the criteria you have for the right person.

A relationship, intimacy, partnership, marriage—all these are about meaningful shifts in life and in consciousness.

'I am no soothsayer or tarot-card reader to be able to tell you when you will meet the right person. But understand the sequence that unfolds in anyone's life. It begins with an inner story and an inner belief. The outward then follows. So, give up the belief that there is a right time to meet what you term as the right person.

'Let us assume that you don't meet someone for the next ten or even twenty years. And that you do meet someone after ten years. Is that too late for you to enter into a relationship? Is 30 too late? Or 40? Or 50? Who is determining the right age for love?

'Society has its own reasons to rush people into marriage. Those reasons hold no logic in today's world. And yet, society says get married before it is too late, before you are too old, before you turn 30, 40 or whatever age. Get married and get it over with.

'Yes, I accept that there is a certain energy and certain age for reproduction. But that is not the be-all and end-all of life. Having children and how and when you seek to have children all depend on your choices in life. Think beyond the restrictions of the world. You shape your narrative. Don't let people around you shape your story. You have to live it. Not them.'

> *Think beyond the restrictions of the world. You shape your narrative. Don't let people around you shape your story. You have to live it. Not them.'*

'Too many people in the West have given up on marriage. They don't understand that it is about developing a mutual admiration for someone, deep respect and trust, awareness of another human's needs.'
—The Dalai Lama

GAUTAM'S GUIDANCE

Each meeting with Gautam was precious, as each one of them gave me rich insight into life, relationships and, eventually, my inner self. Yes, what Gautam asked of me was an effort. There were steps to be followed and work to be done. But his advice had proven effective, simple and practical each time. So, I mentally prepared myself for what he asked me to do. I did it for myself.

The first element to be tackled was the restlessness I was experiencing. Unaddressed, it would snowball and start to affect my physical and emotional wellbeing. Or, god forbid, it could well prove to be the catalyst for another hasty and wrong decision.

Gautam explained to me that restlessness is a big limitation. It drives us to do things in reaction and consume energy and time that could be better spent elsewhere. There is nothing constructive about being driven by restlessness. Yet, overcoming restlessness is neither a matter of keeping busy all the time nor a simple matter of exerting more and more willpower. Something else is needed.

Gautam gave me a two-step blueprint to tackle the restlessness I was experiencing.

The first step was to make others' celebrations and high points celebratory for myself. To show up for others. Not to shy away because I overthink my single status. Not to keep away because I did not have a plus one. Not to stay away because I had not put thought into planning my professional and personal work. Not to attend with the eternal hope that I would meet Mr Right there. I needed to go and be a part of a celebration.

Not simply show up but to plan for it. I was to show up putting my best foot forward, whether in the matter of getting a gift for the occasion or my clothes and the look I wanted.

For instance, a friend's invitation for her tenth wedding anniversary was sent nearly two months in advance. That probably meant my friend was putting a lot of effort and thought into this celebration. She had sent the save-the-date so that her guests could plan in advance too. Sure, the event meant a bit of travel for me, from Delhi to Bangalore. Left to myself, I would probably have sent a gift in my place. But now I was working to plan it out well, figuring out how it could fit into my schedule. The anniversary fell in April, at the start of the new financial year. I could take a day or two off from work and combine it with a weekend and either relaxation or a bit of travel around Bangalore.

The second step was to do something celebratory for myself regularly. Or, as Gautam said, 'Create many, many moments of celebration instead of waiting for the one big celebration in the future, distant in time and reality. Don't become a person who is endlessly waiting to celebrate life, coming alive and truly living for that one special moment or from one special happening to the next. Those are few and far between. When we learn to appreciate and celebrate

Create many, many moments of celebration instead of waiting for the one big celebration in the future, distant in time and reality. Don't become a person who is endlessly waiting to celebrate life.

> *When we learn to appreciate and celebrate the everyday stuff, we build our celebratory muscle. It becomes stronger and stronger and helps us to lift the weight of our lives easily, smoothly and without any injury caused by disappointment, distraction or restlessness.*

the everyday stuff, we build our celebratory muscle. It becomes stronger and stronger and helps us to lift the weight of our lives easily, smoothly and without any injury caused by disappointment, distraction or restlessness.'

So I worked on creating my list of things that felt celebratory to me. Whatever I had deferred and linked to doing after marriage or finding the right person now had a place. I put down the celebratory thing and pinned it to a specific date. I thought about how I could work towards it. If the thought of building a trousseau felt celebratory, I could look at creating a wardrobe now. It called for work and effort—flipping through magazines and browsing looks in stores and online.

Encouraged by Gautam's words, I promised myself that I would tackle all distractions. Restlessness would not lead me to despair or stupid stuff. And I would work on developing my celebratory muscle. I was beginning to understand Gautam's oft repeated words, 'Our inner choices shape our circumstances.'

YOUR SECRET POWERS

PANCH BALA

The Buddha likens the passage of a disciple who has developed the five spiritual powers to that of the mighty River Ganges:

'Similar to the river Ganges, which flows to the East, slopes to the East and inclines to the East, when a disciple develops and pursues the five spiritual powers of faith, effort, mindfulness, concentration and wisdom dependent of seclusion, dependent on dispassion, dependent on cessation, he/she flows, slopes and inclines towards spiritual liberation.'

—The Buddha (*The Samyutta Nikaya*)

Enlightenment may not be your quest. It is possibly only on your bucket list for the next stage of life or the next life. That is fine. But what about happiness? A deep enjoyment of life and all that it holds? Enlightenment is nothing but a state of deep insight into our self, into life and all that life holds. Understanding and insight bring kindness and a better response to people, events and problems. With this more evolved response comes progress. With progress, we experience a new state of positivity and happiness.

The quality of our experiences and lives depends almost entirely on our habits and our response to people and our interactions. We can create and craft a new path if we intentionally create and strengthen these attitudes and qualities in ourselves. This is the start of an upward spiral in our lives. In this upward spiral, we bring focus to our goals and the energy and motivation to get there. Progress follows. Happiness blooms.

No wonder the Buddha refers to these elements of our lives as power. It begins with understanding and acceptance. Let us spend a few moments understanding and accepting these powers that lie waiting within us all in a state of dormancy. Waiting to spring to life with our understanding and effort.

The five spiritual powers the Buddha speaks of are faith, energy, mindfulness, concentration and wisdom.

SADDHA (PALI) OR SHRADDHA (SANSKRIT)

The first power is that of faith or confidence. Faith in whom? Confidence in what?

Confidence in yourself. Confidence in your ability to steer your life the right way. To find solutions and not be overwhelmed by life, people and problems.

Confidence, or faith, is the ability to develop your inner strength and your inner self to create or design your life wisely and intentionally. Confidence is also the trust that your aspirations and desires are not misplaced. It is about overcoming the limiting beliefs that we have all carried since infancy. Confidence that when you reject the trope that it is too good to be true, you will be able to see through it and craft your own good life. Which is not too good to be true for you. Faith and confidence in your own self-worth.

Isn't it interesting that confidence is the opposite of disbelief and mistrust? Most of us are accustomed to seeking help and assistance elsewhere. To have confidence in oneself does not stop anyone from reaching out for support, resources or information, but eventually it all comes down to us, to you.

It is doubt and disbelief in our own selves that stop us from being happy, and cause us to lose time, energy and focus. Doubt leads to the wrong decisions. Doubt springs from that inner space where we lack confidence in ourselves and hold back. The power of faith helps us to confront and move ahead of doubt.

Viriya (Pali) or *virya* (Sanskrit) is the second power of our spirit. Various words try to capture the essence of this

Sanskrit or Pali word: effort, diligence, persistence and energy. Even strength, heroism (from the Indo-Iranian root to be brave or be a hero) or enthusiasm. Another interpretation is the unbegrudging, glad or enthusiastic effort that we put into our lives to progress. The Buddha's teachings are clear: true progress comes through wholesome actions and wholesome choices. The *kusala*, or the skilful. To put in energy and diligence to rob a bank, for instance, is unwholesome and not viriya.

The Buddha's teachings are all about a longer-term perspective. To start an extramarital relationship, an affair is not wholesome. Whatever is not wholesome may bring us some enjoyment and pleasure in the short term. It will, however, then create stress, stop or delay progress on other goals, distract from other priorities, and eventually lead to unhappiness rather than the anticipated happiness.

In the times of the Buddha, viriya also meant a great warrior's strength in overcoming one's enemies. The strongest enemy is lack of will or laziness in doing what we need to do when we need to do it. In the modern world, it is also distraction. On one level, viriya is the ability to take 'heroic' action, control laziness, and on the other, it is about focus and remaining undistracted.

Effort as a spiritual power especially works to develop the *kusala*, wholesome and skilled mental states. The Buddha gives an example of those who exercise effort. They will never postpone or avoid correct and wholesome actions with excuses such as: it is too cold; it is too hot; it is too early; it is too late; I am hungry; I have just eaten; I have to embark on a journey; or I am tired after travelling.

Because this effort stems from inner motivation, we have the energy to sustain it. The energy to persist. It is effort that leads us closer to our wholesome goals and creates the momentum for progress. An approach that is free of resentment, of begrudging effort and of giving it 100 per cent. A definition from the *Abhidharma-samuccaya* asks the question and answers: 'What is virya? It is the mind intent on being ever-active, devoted, unshaken, not turning back and being indefatigable. It perfects and realizes what is conducive to the positive.'

Sati (Pali) or *smriti* (Sanskrit) is the third *bala,* or the third strength. Awareness, mindfulness and the recall (*smriti)* to be mindful. To be mindful and aware of the sensations and needs of the body (*kayanupassana).* To be mindful, aware and honest about the emotions and feelings that arise within (*vedananupassana*). To be mindful of the mind (*cittaanupassana)*—honest self-reflection. What am I experiencing? Is my mind focused and calm? Distracted or disturbed? And, lastly, contemplation and mindfulness of the code of conduct, *dharma*, or *dhamma* in Pali (*dhammaanupassana*).

Mindfulness is awareness. Awareness of the now. Awareness of yourself and what is important to you. For instance, if it is important to you to remain healthy and fit, then you have to be mindful of getting enough exercise, your diet, and getting enough sunlight and sleep. So every time you skip your exercise regime, whatever it may be, you are mindful that it is taking you away from your dhamma, your priority and your code of conduct.

It is mindfulness that keeps you centred in the now. Away from regrets of the past and vague hopes for the future. It is mindfulness that helps you heal from past heartbreak. It is mindfulness that allows you to move ahead with a clear mind about what needs to be done for yourself and your growth. It is mindfulness that will allow you to make the most of Gautam's guidance. The use of the highlighter in this book is a tool of mindfulness. Your notes in the margin will serve as a reminder to recall.

To live in a state of mindlessness is to ask for trouble sooner rather than later. Mindlessness creates conditions for poor decision-making and, therefore, regret. Poor decision-making creates conditions for loss—loss of time, loss of energy, loss of money, loss of self-confidence. And even the loss of opportunity. The power of mindfulness (*sati*) is able to oppose and control mindlessness, or heedlessness. Mindfulness also brings a balance between faith and wisdom, between effort and concentration.

Samadhi bala (Pali and Sanskrit) is the fourth power that you have. Traditionally, it is the power of concentration (samadhi). Deep concentration. In today's world, this is the power to remain focused and undistracted. This is the age of distraction. Supreme distraction. And modern humanity leads an interrupted existence. Interrupted by devices. By lifestyle choices. By physical and mental noise. By work and the workplace. By social media. By gaming. By streaming. By the World Wide Web. By browsing.

Distraction cannot lead to progress. It is the difference between being destiny-driven versus destination-driven. A clear destination and a non-distracted journey. Without both, we cannot experience steady progress. Progress is not linked to the large milestones of life but to the smaller achievements that are possible on a daily or weekly basis.

The Buddha explained that to bring out focus and concentration is actually to do away with sensual desire *(kamacchanda)*, ill-will *(vyapada)*, laziness and sloth *(thina middha)*, restlessness and remorse *(uddacca kukkucca)*, and doubt *(vicikicca)*.

Those who work to develop focus *(vitakka)* are not only able to start something new very well but are also able to sustain it *(vicara)*. This sustained focus brings joy *(piti)*. From joy arises happiness *(sukha)*. From happiness emerges focus and confidence *(ekaggata* and *upekkha)*.

Doing away with sensual desire has to be understood deeply. You may well ask: If sensual desire is being done away with, then what is the point of the book? After all, it is all about creating and manifesting what you need and want, perhaps even long for, in order to enjoy your life.

It falls into place when we understand that the Buddha refers to doing away with craving rather than desire. Craving, or *tanha*, is the unending thirst that we can fall prey to. More and more. More sensory stimuli and more sensual pleasure. And a feeling that nothing is enough. Nothing is fulfilling or satisfactory.

Being ruled by craving and longing is also a distraction. It does not allow for focus. To do so is to feel unfulfilled all the time. As you work on focus and concentration, you feel more fulfilled. More settled. When you know what is enough, you are happy.

The power of concentration, or samadhi, is able to oppose and control distraction.

Panna (Pali) and *prajna* (Sanskrit) is the last and final power, that of wisdom. The four powers of confidence, effort, mindfulness and focus naturally lead to wisdom. In that sense, wisdom is very hard-won. And yet it needs a certain wisdom to be able to exercise the first four powers. The wisdom that the Buddha referred to is not knowledge or rote learning. It is insight. An intuitive understanding that arises from close observation of experience.

The spiritual power of wisdom (*panna*) is able to oppose and control ignorance.

Gaining and growing in these spiritual powers requires commitment and good company. If the company you keep undermines the commitment you have to yourself and your journey, the powers remain dormant. Within. But out of reach.

Ultimately, the company we keep and the partner or partners we choose in the course of a lifetime are vital to our being able to develop and work on these powers mindfully and wisely.

'By endeavour, diligence, discipline and self-mastery, let the wise man make (of himself) an island that no flood can overwhelm.'

—The Buddha (*The Dhammapada*)

WISPS OF DOUBT!

SHAPING MY NARRATIVE

'The third form of awareness is awareness
of thoughts. You are aware when your
thoughts are filled with desire; and you are
aware when your thoughts are empty of
desire.

As you observe thoughts in this manner,
you understand that thoughts continually
come into being and pass away. This
understanding concentrates the mind and
enables the mind to become self-sufficient,
not grasping at external objects'.

—The Buddha (*Maha Satipatthana Sutra*)

A handful of good friends tried to set me up with a possible
Mr Right. They were aided by algorithms that trawled the
stratosphere of the net and databases that tried to correlate
lives. Dad looked through newspaper ads and made a few
suggestions, even as my amusement at his choices made him
fume.

Nothing was working out. True, I was relaxed. True, I
was happy. True, I had overcome a huge restlessness. True, I
was successful. This was a good time in my life. A good space
to be in. I had earned it. But strangely, the world around me
saw things differently.

Even when I drove my swanky new car with panache.
Even when I dressed with care. Even when I showed up at
parties and get-togethers. But I didn't do it with the ulterior
motive of bumping into Mr Right or even Mr Almost Right. I

showed up to bond with friends, to relax, and to enjoy good conversation and good food in great environments. I showed up to celebrate life.

Some whispered. Then many voices coalesced. They spoke as one, like sibilant Nagini. They murmured and hissed that the time was past. Women did not really get married at 38, 39 or even later. Compromise was the solution. I should choose someone, choose anyone and just get married. I should lower my standards—all the good ones were taken, all the good ones were married, all the good ones were already out of reach and so many wouldn't really consider marriage to me.

Why not, I wondered.

Oh, because you have a messy record. Oh, because you aren't reed-thin. Oh, because you are out-earning most men. Oh, because you have opinions and a loud voice. Oh, because you are actually successful. Oh, because the 'big 40' is on the horizon. Oh, because you aren't really the domestic and settled kind. Oh, because your traumatic experiences haven't made you humble. Oh, because you still expect that you won't have to compromise, and that is downright insulting to life. Oh, because you are too good-looking, chances are you will be unfaithful after marriage. Oh, because you are happy, which means there is something wrong with you. Oh, because you are a rebel. Oh, because it appears that you may have a problem adjusting to a traditional family. Oh, because you earn well, but the huge pots of inherited wealth are missing. Oh, because you don't fit into any moulds. Oh, because you've had PCOD. Oh, because you think that you are equal to any man. Oh, because at 38 or 39, how will you have children? Oh, because you dare to dream. Oh, because Oh, because . . . just because.

Perhaps it was just because I existed. Maybe it rankled that I did it despite the experiences I had had.

The effort to rise had been back-breaking but worth every single drop of the blood, sweat and tears it had taken.

The effort to rise was rewarding. It was an effort to make something of myself and to live life for my own sake. I had come to understand that my life was important and that I was worth it. Truly worth it. Far more than any beauty brand could understand.

Perhaps it was a symptom of my naivety, but I had genuinely believed that others would feel happy for me. That my story was inspiring and that people around me would find it so.

Wisps of doubt had started to swirl around me. It is not karma that is a bitch, but the ugliness of doubt. Doubt, whether from within or without, is insidious and erosive. It stops us from living our lives. It stops us from believing in our own capabilities. It stops us from taking steps to transform our lives. Doubt robs us of our dreams and hopes.

I had held fast to my beliefs and my dreams. My dreams of possibilities unfolding in my life. My dreams of a fulfilled life. True, I was neither incomplete without the right life partner nor unfulfilled. But I did think having the right life partner was part of it all. Some part of me sought to create a family. Be a part of one. Was I on the right path?

If left unattended, these doubts would soon become snares, lethal enough to hold me back. They were sharp and dangerous enough to prevent me from believing, dreaming and working in the direction that I sought.

I needed help. There was only one thing to do.

Gautam agreed to meet me early in the morning on the coming Sunday. I was delighted that I was going to be meeting him. It had been a while, after all. I was less than delighted to be asked to meet him at 5.30 a.m. But he insisted that it was the only time he was available, and since the days were getting warmer, he was choosing less and less to step out during the day. Plus, he was really busy at other times. I had no say over the time or his choice of an outdoor venue. But I could make it easier and more palatable by making it into a bit of a picnic.

I pulled into the parking lot of the fabulous Lodhi Gardens at 5.20 a.m. I had packed a food hamper and carried it with me. I thought I had done well putting it all together. While the early morning was a deterrent to a full meal, conversations with Gautam took time and ranged over an easy couple of hours. The spread would serve well as an early morning breakfast at the end of our walk-talkathon.

Gautam chose vegetarian food options without noisily proclaiming himself a vegetarian. I had observed this and made a careful note of it while inviting him or eating with him at any point in time. Each interaction with Gautam over a meal was interesting—he did not have the full three meals plus that most of us had. He usually limited himself to one meal a day, sometimes extending it to two. He ate with a quiet enjoyment and gratitude that was somehow inspiring to observe.

I laid out my carefully chosen spread. A thermos of tea, piping hot and gently aromatic. A loaf of artisanal bread, which could be sliced and eaten as was or slathered with the strawberry jam I had made and bottled just last weekend. Homemade vegetable cutlets of two kinds and a small bottle of homemade coriander and mint chutney. A small, indulgent chocolate cake that I'd ordered from a friend who was a home baker. Slices of hard yet sweet melon. A bunch of tempting-looking grapes, carefully washed and dried. A few bananas and some fresh strawberries. Given the walk and the rising temperature, the few bottles of water were more of a necessity than a luxury. I hoped my selection would be tempting for him and something he would enjoy.

I found myself wishing for the predictable red-and-white checked picnic blanket to spread on the grass. But I had brought two thick bedspreads and two large cushions. The food was carefully packed in a large basket. Another basket carried mugs, some cutlery, small disposable plates and paper napkins.

I tried a few calf and leg stretches, knowing fully well that once Gautam got there, I would need warmed-up muscles just to keep up with him. He could set a pace that pushed me a few shades beyond my comfort zone.

My phone pinged. Gautam was in the parking lot, looking for me. Soon, we were on our walk-talkathon. Sure enough, our pace made me glad for the bottle of water I had kept in my small crossbody sling bag. And the chewing gum I was already popping into my mouth. Hopefully, it would all make the walk easier for me to handle, and I wouldn't huff and puff my way through it.

Gautam heard me out with his characteristic patience. The very act of him listening to me intently calmed me down. From him, I was learning that listening was every bit as powerful as speaking. Many times more so.

'GP, why are you allowing these voices from around you to disturb you in any way? It is okay. Let them say or think what they like. I've told you earlier—you are scripting this narrative. You are creating your own experiences. You are the creator. If you buy into the stories that people are telling you, the whole story of **your** life starts being crafted by **them**. Is that what you want? Keep the power of your own life with you. Keep these people and their stuff as far away as you possibly can. Or don't allow it to disturb you.'

'I may not be strong enough, Gautam. I don't know how to keep these voices and these people at bay. What should I do, and how should I go about it? Do you think the force of these opinions in my life is because I am a woman? Would this be any different if I were a man?'

'Well, GP, let me answer that last one first. Yes, it is more so because you are a woman. But men have similar experiences. Doubts have a way of slithering into our hearts. And sometimes it is difficult to tell whether the small voice within is because of voices outside or our own disbelief and doubt.'

I was taken aback and asked, 'Really? Are you sure that men have a similar campaign of doubt and disbelief? A lot of things in a man's life are geared towards giving him more and more confidence. Men seem to have a head start in the race for confidence. Women are better at second-guessing themselves and seeking someone to appreciate them so that we become and feel more confident in ourselves.'

There was a wealth of understanding in Gautam's response: 'Men's lived reality, or their experience, is different from women's, no doubt. But the human experience, the human struggle and the human story are alike, GP. They are not very different.

'For instance, a man in your situation would equally experience loneliness and the absence of a special someone, a companion by their side. They may have moments of awkwardness while entering a party or a social gathering. They may also have been warned to get married before the receding hairline and the advancing tummy spoil their chances. They, too, may be seeking the right companion or a great friend.

'The only difference is that men are not falsely trained to equate their worth with marriage. Their false narrative is different—it is about sexual prowess; it is increasingly about being cool and polished while holding on to sensitivity and being a great listener. It is about having washboard abs. It is about being confident, manly and strong. It is about being romantic and understanding all the time. It is about being supportive in every way—financially, emotionally and practically. It is about job performance, success and carving an upward trajectory in life. It is almost always about earning well before they can think about getting married.

'The world as a whole criticizes a man's decision to marry or to start living with someone before he is financially sound. Take it from me that men are also experiencing something like this in society. Perhaps the intensity and ferocity of it are a bit more muted. Perhaps it starts much later for men than for women. And of course, men don't have the same pressure from the biological clock ticking away. But the force of societal pressure is there.

'The fact is, our environment plays out these doubts and insecurities. And because the germ of this doubt exists within us, we are quick to accept the voices as being true. And that is how our narrative is shaped—by the twin forces of our own disbelief and the voices of doubt in the world. Once you buy into the societal narrative, you create your experiences in accord with it. And reality mimics the beliefs inside. Forget people. Check in with yourself. Be clear about what you want!'

The silence between us stretched and spun out. I needed to understand how to shape my own narrative. I needed to create the experiences that I wished for. Without any interference. Without any static. Without any doubt.

So I asked Gautam, 'How do I shape my own narrative in this case, Gautam? How does anyone do it? What is required and how do I go about it?'

Gautam said, 'Your past experiences and relationships and the people around you are deep influences. A set of underlying beliefs drives our lives. If negative or limiting beliefs persist, you will continue to have bad or toxic dating experiences and difficult relationships, and you will continue to attract the same kind of people to you.

Setting your intent and bringing focus and intentionality into this search for a partner is the first step to making it happen. Do this when all else is well and when you have already established the foundation of happiness within yourself.

'Setting your intent and bringing focus and intentionality into this search for a partner is the first step to making it happen. Do this when all else is well and when you have already established the foundation of happiness within yourself. I see you have already done that. Now start out on your journey to find love, not because you are incomplete without it but because you are open to it, because you have much to share and much to offer to love and to loving relationships.

'You must seek love not out of desperation or neediness nor because of incompleteness. Not because you need someone's money nor because you need to escape the circumstances of your life. Not because they offer a way out. But **because** you are calm, successful, happy and in a good space to grow along with another human being. Because you're able to support their growth as well as your personal growth.'

I was quiet. My body was solely focused on keeping pace with Gautam and my mind on understanding this powerful life lesson. How could I use the power of self-belief to my advantage in life? In the matter of marriage? In the matter of successful relationships? And how could I use intention to bring about—to literally manifest—what I desired?

> 'Develop yourself. Use desire as a catalyst for growth. Understand the nature of life and how the universe works. People and relationships are not the means to an end. Age has nothing to do with marriage. Complete yourself as a human being.'
>
> —Naveena Reddi (in a personal chat)

GAUTAM'S GUIDANCE

Gautam shared with me the profound truth that we are continually shaping and creating our own lives. Our experiences are conceived within the belly, the womb of our beliefs. Our beliefs shape our response to life, define our decisions and form our choices. Like the decision tree, each response, each decision and each choice continually shapes or leads to the next. And reinforces the truth of the belief that gave rise to it all.

Our experiences are conceived within the belly, the womb of our beliefs. Our beliefs shape our response to life, define our decisions and form our choices. Like the decision tree, each response, each decision and each choice continually shapes or leads to the next. And reinforces the truth of the belief that gave rise to it all. This is our power as the creators of our own lives. This is the underlying truth of **Aham Brahmasmi.**

This is our power as the creators of our own lives. This is the underlying truth of *Aham Brahmasmi*.

Our doubt and disbelief hold us back. And we create our experiences and our reality accordingly. Faith, confidence, hope and belief all work together to shape a different reality. Holding on to faith and belief in the face of a reality that disappoints that faith and mocks that belief is difficult. But it is entirely necessary to bring about the change we want and the results we long for. When faith and belief are shaken, the future of our dreams is shaken.

Action and response follow an underlying belief. And results follow the action and response. If we are unhappy with our lives or the lack of results in one area of life, or if we feel stuck and helpless, it is time to turn inward and examine the underlying beliefs in that area of life.

Gautam paraphrased Japanese thought leader Dr Daikasu Ikeda's line on bringing about internal change by recognizing, challenging (to change) and working to overcome. Though Dr Ikeda speaks in the context of world peace, this formula holds true in our lives. If limiting beliefs are holding us back, we need to take the first step by accepting that. We must understand and identify or, as Dr Ikeda says, 'recognize', that limiting belief.

This recognition, identification and acceptance start when we experience the pain and frustration of a deadlock. And we are forced to find solutions and seek answers. Ultimately, our reason to change our paradigm simply has to be stronger than our reason to stay the same.

The first step is taking time out—with ourselves. A pen and paper are handy, but even handier is uninterrupted space to calm ourselves and think about the underlying belief holding us back.

Gautam mentioned some common limiting beliefs and paradigms about how life is, how we are and what we deserve. These are:

1. Life is all about compromise.
2. No one gets it all or has it all. Very few have it all. Like the lines from the famous song '*Kabhi kisiko mukammal jahan nahin milta. Kabhi zameen toh kabhi asmaan nahin milta.*' (No one ever gets a complete world. Sometimes the earth is missing, and sometimes it's the sky).

3. It is too good to be true / I am not deserving (of what is too good to be true) / I am not worthy of having this desire / dream fulfilled.
4. I am too old for _____ OR I am too young for _____
5. It will never be _____ / I will never be _____
6. No matter what I do, I could always do better.
7. Life has always been hard on me. Therefore, _____
8. I shouldn't have to work for this. Life is supposed to either make it easy for me or very difficult for me. Either way, I am not required to work on it.

Whatever your poison (of belief), it is possible to replace it once it is identified.

Start by writing down what you are seeking. That big dream. That right person. The right life for yourself. And watch—the belief that holds you back in that area of life will slither out from the dark holes within. Its role is to keep you convinced that it won't work out for you. It often does so in a voice of reason and rationale—this is not how life works; this is not how it will work for you; you have to be realistic; you are not so lucky; learn to be satisfied; everyone has to compromise and so on.

Now create the opposite voice. Go all out. Replace each element of that limiting belief and start moving to the other end of the spectrum of beliefs. If the belief is about life being a compromise, then craft a belief about abundance and completion. If it is about how no one gets it all or has it all, then look around at those who have full and complete lives and repeatedly tell the mind that it is possible. Grab it by its neck and tell it differently. Take the opposite position. Keep affirming this new belief to yourself.

Most limiting beliefs withdraw when faced with a clear affirmation. They retreat further when you start to write and revisit that writing from time to time.

Let your list of what you are looking for be clear. Be precise. Be expansive. Be exhaustive. It is your canvas to paint as you desire. Don't let the demons of doubt and disbelief hold you back. Here are some examples:

1. Life is how you choose to make it. And I make mine abundant, complete and fulfilled. I open myself to the limitless possibility of finding my right life partner.
2. I don't have to recreate the reality of the song. I can and am empowered to recreate my own reality. It is possible to have a complete life. I need to know and work on the ways in which I make my reality complete. I now work on the ways to make my reality complete.
3. I am worthy, and I am abundant.
4. What has my age got to do with anything? Even if I marry well and add to my happiness at 50 or 60, it is fine. No rush. There is no time or defined age for a happy marriage or companionship for life.

Gautam shared with me the importance of writing out a plan for what I was seeking in life. Writing leaves an imprint not only on paper but on our most important organ—our brain. When you write, the brain goes to work thinking of ways and means of getting you there.

Emotions, no matter their intensity and baggage, don't make the cut to propel us forward. It is writing, clarity of goals and a calm working at

> *Emotions, no matter their intensity and baggage, don't make the cut to propel us forward. It is writing, clarity of goals and a calm working at them that does it. This momentum is our progress and the secret of happiness.*

them that does it. This momentum is our progress and the secret of happiness.

Doubt fades in the face of our confidence and the depth of our belief that we are scripting our story by understanding the laws of life, creating a calm certainty about life, having the willingness to change, and taking the right steps to work on those goals.

The flip side of doubt is fear. Watch out for that fear. Understand it. Do you fear that if you find someone wonderful in another part of the country or the world, how will you look after your father? Do you fear that the world will laugh at you getting married at 36, 39, 42 or 50? Do you fear the consequences if the marriage does not turn out well? Do you fear juggling a career, caring for your father, and managing a new relationship?

Gautam was right. There was an underlying fear in my heart. My disbelief stemmed from the fear of repeating the negative experiences of my past. It stemmed from my desire to look after my father and, at the same time, carve out my own path and progress in life.

Gautam's words gave me courage and a new understanding that I could move beyond my past. I could move ahead. I could make the passage and travel the road I created. I could progress. It was doable. It was possible. My belief and my efforts would make it possible.

A SLICE OF MAGIC!

MANIFESTING LOVE

'All (mental) states have mind as their forerunner,
mind is their chief and they are mind-made.
If one speaks or acts with a pure mind, happiness
follows one as one's shadow that does not
leave one.'

—The Buddha

I had called it off with Raj.

Oh, let me take you a page or two back. I had met Raj through a site, and we hit it off from the word go. Our first telephone conversation started around 10 p.m., and we reluctantly ended it around 3 a.m.

Yes, there was intensity here. Yes, he had travelled from Bangalore to Delhi to meet me for three, or was it four, successive weekends. Yes, he had formally proposed. Yes, he had met my dad. Yes, he wined and dined me just so. Yes, he courted me very, very well.

'But,' the little voice within said, 'he is not quite right for me.' This would not end in my happily ever after. There were too many highs and lows in the interactions and in the endless phone calls. It would be a rough ride despite the sizzle, the charm and the boxes checked. Despite my own need to get on with this aspect of life.

That phone call at around 1 a.m. after the conclusion of the *India Today Conclave* was not easy. But I had to tell him that it wasn't working out for me. And given the geographical distance, a call was the only way. I didn't want him to travel to Delhi before sharing my point of view.

It was not easy. We had covered ground so quickly and had started building on hopes for a shared tomorrow. But this time I listened to my gut—that voice of intuition. And followed through. With calmness and composure.

There was a calm certainty within me that life would become what I painted on its canvas with my dreams and desires. I would find love and stability. The care and love that I had given to my parents and others would return to me.

Tulika had found a profile that impressed her very much. She had been on my case to write in and get in touch with Manu. She described him as a wonderful human being based on her understanding of his profile and his picture on the portal. And she hadn't bothered to hide her impatience and annoyance while I pursued my relationship with Raj.

But I was clear about one thing: I would not explore two profiles at the same time. There would be closure on one before the next. Either a yea or a nay. One profile, one person, one life. I would not choose the path of looking at and comparing people and lives. I wasn't window-shopping. Nor was I holding out for the best opportunity by comparing notes on height, weight, bank balance . . . whatever was bundled up.

With closure on Raj, I felt free to reach out to Tulika's highly and fiercely recommended Manu. He responded quite promptly to my message to him, and we fixed a time for a meet at the spanking-new Radisson Hotel in Noida.

He had shrugged off my suggestion to meet on 15 March, which was a holiday. I wasn't happy about being asked to meet on a working day, but the meeting was deferred to the 16th, a Thursday, with the onus on me to call once I left office. Why couldn't he do the chivalrous bit and take it on himself to call me and check? Was this a precursor to a mismatch? Well, only the meeting ahead would reveal that. I chose to go through with it despite some misgivings.

I had barely walked into the hotel lobby and picked up my phone to call him when I saw a tall, lean man wearing a navy-blue collared T-shirt cross the lobby. And somehow, he turned and looked at me even before the phone rang. As a smile broke over his face, magic flashed in the air like a crackle of fire or a bolt of lightning. A hum, a flash and something indescribable . . .

Pleasant . . . there was something just so pleasant about him. The cup of coffee stretched on. Conversation flowed, and so did time. He was not suave. He was sincere. He was not textbook handsome. He had a receding hairline. He was not rolling in wealth. He had created a business, was running it successfully and was looking after his family well. He was not flirtatious. He was careful with people. Having never been married, he wanted companionship and family. He was not dishy; he was the guy next door. He was not dreamy. He had dreams for his future.

I declined staying back for dinner as it was getting late and Yusuf, my driver, darn him, was unwell. And strangely, it simply did not occur to me to send Yusuf away and drive myself back. Crazy me . . .

Would the parting promise to meet again culminate in the next meeting? Was it just a platitude? Was he interested? Would he connect over a call or send a message? Would love unfold from here on? Or was this just a pleasant interlude? A pleasant blind date?

I could feel the restlessness start to build within. Again and yet again, I checked my messages, turning up the ringer on the phone. What would Friday bring? I had to struggle to remain focused and productive at work. The undercurrent of restlessness had to be managed with discipline and sheer love of work and being a part of this buzzing media conglomerate.

I dutifully told Tulika that she was right. I had really enjoyed meeting Manu. But to her natural curiosity as to when we were planning on meeting again, I had no answer. I had not heard back from him. Friday rolled over, and Saturday flew by with my usual household chores and a weekly massage. I got my massage in the old-fashioned way by an old-fashioned *maalishwali* who trudged in faithfully early on Saturday mornings. I slept through most of her halfhearted pressing of my legs and feet.

Saturday was nearly over; my chores were done and I had checked all the boxes, including spending time with my dad. To get my mind off the silent phone, I decided to use all the strawberries in the fridge to make some sort of dessert. As I flicked through some of my mom's cookbooks, I thought how strange it is that impatience hums its crescendo and slows time down to an unbearable crawl.

Oh, what the heck! If he wouldn't call, why could I not? What was the code of conduct holding me back? What was wrong with my reaching out? Would he read it as desperation? Or decide that I was not worth pursuing just because I made the first move? Even though my employer published *Cosmopolitan* magazine, I was not going to start on its much-followed advice on who makes which move. I was interested; I would follow up, and if anyone decided to misread my sincere interest, it was on them.

I could hear the smile and the pleasure in his voice. He was on his way to attend someone's wedding reception. What was I doing? I was making a strawberry something and would be happy to share it with him if he decided to show up. Ah, embarrassment . . . Had I goofed up? Was I being too forward? We could meet for dinner on Sunday evening, he said.

I agreed. Since this **was** an extension of a blind date, I followed through on my own peculiar code of playing it safe and did not share my address. He would pick me up on Sunday evening outside Sector 37. I was deliberately vague about where I lived.

The day flew by. A quick dash to the salon. A coat of nail paint. A face pack for some glow. Nail biting—despite the new coat of nail paint—indecision over clothes. Staring at the open closet as if something would happen magically.

A second hair wash? God . . . I felt dizzy and excited. Dating was its own pleasure. Its own high. What was the need to add anything further to the mix of that pleasure, the bubbling excitement and the effervescence of it all? I certainly needed nothing more.

My phone pinged. Manu was on his way. I was already dashing for the main door and making sure to triple-lock and secure the house. My dad was in bed by 7.30 p.m. Playing by the same safety norms, I dutifully informed Tulika and left a detailed note for my dad on the dining table.

Anticipation. A slow lick of heat within. A curl of warmth at the look in his eyes. The sizzle was back that Sunday evening. Had it ever left? It was probably on a delicious simmer. The evening flew on silken wings. Possibilities stretched their yearning arms. My only regret was choosing Italian food with its characteristic lingering garlicky notes. What if there was a kiss to complete the evening?

Strangely, my desire for chewing gum was answered when I spotted the plump blocks of Wrigley's Watermelon in the open console of his car. We were on our way back after a dinner on the open-air terrace of Big Chill in Khan Market. The slight nip of the evening air melted away, as did time. Even the silence in the car strummed and shimmered with passion. I knew my cheeks and ears felt hot. We would meet again, and soon.

There was a sparkle to the next morning. The Monday morning blues had disappeared. This Monday bubbled and danced. I thought I probably did as well. With the financial year coming to an end, my team and I were snowed under with work. Appraisals needed to be carried out and budgets formulated. Effort put into the incentives for the current year and the next. And, of course, there was the entire process of giving increments and promotions.

The business had grown rapidly, and new magazines were launching at a dizzying pace. Work had grown, as had the entire organization and the Board's expectations from the human resources team. It was a long day, and I got back late that evening. I managed a few minutes with Dad. Then I warmed up my dinner, and settled down for my journalling, prayers and chanting.

The sudden message from Manu at around 9.30 p.m. was surprising. As was his insistence that I come down to meet him. Curiouser still was the one line that he hadn't been able to concentrate on his work the whole day.

Surely, I could be forgiven the smug smile and the quickened heartbeat. A quick wash. A careless flick of the comb. A smoothing on of lipstick. The ritual of locks and the key tucked safely into my cross-body sling bag. A sprint to the main gate of Sector 37. Only to reach it simultaneously with him. Murmured hellos. And silence. A sudden shyness bloomed.

'Let me take you for a drive,' he said in his attractive voice. The night was young, but no one knew I was out with him. I had not left a note for Dad, nor had I messaged Tulika. My safety net was not in place. I felt a sudden uneasiness, so I pulled out my phone and messaged Tulika. Then I breathed a little easier.

Manu swung away from the main city and headed to the expressway. It was fairly new and not a very familiar part of the city I had lived in for the past 6 years. Other cars whizzed by reassuringly. Strains of music floated around us as the FM station played in a murmur. The evening had taken on a surreal feel.

The stop was sudden. He pulled up on the side of the expressway. Left the engine running. He pointed out a new and fashionable condo complex, naming it. He turned to face me fully. His gaze was deep yet unreadable. I was uncertain about the stop and what Manu wanted to convey. 'Yeah. I know this place. I toyed with the idea of buying an apartment here last year. Somehow, I didn't follow through.'

He reached out to push back the hair strand falling over my face. There was a surprising warmth and gentleness in his touch. 'Hmm . . . My brother-in-law had booked an apartment here for me. And how I wish I had held on to it! If I had, we could have lived here after marriage.'

> 'From our past thoughts comes our present state of mind. From our present thoughts will come our future state of mind. Our life is the creation of our minds.'
>
> —The Buddha (ascribed)

THE SKILL OF COMPATIBILITY

'The moon, the sun and my teaching . . .
They all shine brightly when they are uncovered.'

—The Buddha (*The Numerical Discourses*)

Modern research firmly places happiness as a skill that is acquired as the result of a series of actions and choices in life, thought and relationships. It posits happiness as an approach and attitude that can be learned.

Of course, the Buddha said all this and more some 2500 years ago. He said that happiness comes from choosing the skillful (*kusala*) or applying skillful remedies (*upaya kusala*) to different areas of life. We can choose the skilful, the helpful and the positive only when we live with awareness. This means living with intent and mindfulness.

Remedies (*upaya*) for what, you might ask. Remedies to *dukkha,* the suffering of life—its stress, pain, disappointment and sense of dissatisfaction. The feeling that life is unsatisfactory. The antidote to that *dukkha* is the remedy, or *upaya*.

Remedies can be chosen or created and then acted upon. It all depends on our understanding of this sequence and our willingness to act on it. The process starts with making the right choice.

This holds true for remedies for OUR romantic life too. The Buddha knew just how vital it is to make the right choice in companions and to choose close associates well. The importance of making the 'right' choice directly impacts our peace and happiness and the longevity of our relationships. How, then, can we 'skilfully' choose our life partner? Discussed and scattered throughout the *Sutta Pitaka* (the Basket of Discourse) are the steps that help us choose wisely and well.

STEP ONE: BEYOND TRADITIONAL THOUGHT, BEYOND TRADITIONAL CRITERIA

India's heritage has largely been a matter of tradition, which can become rigid, get straitjacketed and even devolve into righteousness. The life and teachings of the Buddha are marked by questioning tradition and going beyond tradition. Shrugging off blind acceptance. The Buddha was known to choose his own path. He was known for his experiments to distinguish right from wrong. He encouraged his followers to leave aside race, caste, gender and external appearance when choosing or selecting those in close relationships.

We can extend this thought and the underlying skill to choose and accept a partner. The Buddha would never advise his lay disciples to choose a partner **only** from their own caste, race or creed. He pointed out the absolute importance of compatibility in attitude and approach to life. He spoke of the risk of forming partnerships or intimate relationships with those who were immature. *He termed* those who were not yet fully developed in their thought and approach as *bala*. On the other hand, he encouraged close relationships and partnerships with those who were mature, wise and thinking individuals, the *pandita*.

STEP 2: BEYOND FIRST IMPRESSIONS AND BEYOND APPEARANCE

The twenty-first century lends itself to multiple choices. From the humble toothpaste to the uber-luxurious vacation, we are spoiled for choice. The plenitude is confusing. Bewildering.

Somehow, each aspect of modern life is about getting more, having more and being more. Media, movies and books have shaped a culture that emphasizes good looks, youth and a glittering presentation. Our culture has a huge bias for 'better-looking' people, irrespective of other elements.

Looks and presentation then add up to the overemphasis on sexual quotient and appeal. Photoshopped and touched-up images have impressed on us the need for partners who look just right. All of us, men or women, are vulnerable to this bias in our society. Media and social conditioning have led us all to believe that the better-looking our partner, the more desirable-looking our partner, the greater our happiness in having them as our partner. The reality is that appearance alone ensures neither happiness nor longevity in relationships.

A better and deeper understanding of those we wish to associate with is necessary. It is important to go beyond the first impression and beyond appearances.

> Neither their appearance nor a brief positive
> Impression depicts a true picture of people.
> —The Buddha (*The Connected Discourses*)

STEP 3: UNDERSTANDING THROUGH ASSOCIATION, OBSERVATION AND EVALUATION

So, how do we then understand people better? Understanding comes from spending time with another. From observing their behaviour and actions, their interactions. From an unprejudiced evaluation of their beliefs and lives. Since the basis of strong and healthy relationships is a better understanding of people, it needs time and wisdom. Using skill, wisdom and understanding (*pannavata* in Pali). To better observe and evaluate the inner state or inner development of others. And then choose to be with them.

This process is important to understand your compatibility. Compatibility matters when you decide on a committed relationship with someone. This could well be at work, in a business partnership or in a personal relationship. If all you are seeking is fun, pleasure, a hookup, a fleeting transaction or just someone to have around for the short term, then compatibility is a lesser matter. When it comes to the long term, compatibility is vital.

In the modern world, we all have somehow come to accept and understand that compatibility is a mutual liking—maybe for poetry or Thai curry. Or knowing a similar set of things or people. Or having a similar net worth. Of course, if these things happen, it is wonderful. And yet, compatibility is more than checking boxes.

It is more than a shared liking for a certain kind of movies or food, and goes beyond belonging to a similar social and financial background. Compatibility is more than having similar jobs in the same industry. It is about shared values and an approach to life that you can respect, appreciate and sometimes even learn from.

What, then, is compatibility? The Buddha taught his followers the four elements of compatibility. All the elements have a similar set of values and priorities. What is important to both people in the relationship. These are:

1. A shared approach to spiritual development: if the term 'spirituality' confuses the issue, this can be better understood as 'self-development'. It signifies a similar approach to progress in the non-tangible areas of life. What is the approach of each partner in the relationship to moving ahead and working on self-development? Do they respect each other's approach at the same time?

2. A similar respect for self-discipline: this is an important facet of compatibility. If one partner is given to great self-discipline in matters of health and physical fitness and the other is totally unconcerned, it can grow them apart over time. If one takes responsibility for doing well

professionally and the other is indifferent, then too the possibility of a gap exists. The management of time and the use of devices are points to observe and evaluate. How does the other use their time? Is it a balanced or a lopsided approach? This is key to their self-discipline.

3. A similar respect for giving, sharing and charity: If the two partners are on two different planes of giving or sharing, there is an imbalance. This refers to the ability to share and to give time, resources, energy and even charity. It encompasses the approach to caregivers and those less fortunate, as well as the approach to staff and juniors.

4. A similar level of understanding and wisdom: This does not refer to intellectual attainment or educational degrees. It **does** refer to the mental vibe. An understanding of life and its priorities that is on a similar plane. It encompasses skill, intellect, emotional maturity, attitude, reason and knowledge. For success in any long-term relationship, a similar level of understanding and respect for the other's wisdom is vital.

These criteria are as much about you as they are about the other. No one can understand or assess another person's approach to self-development without first understanding their own. You cannot observe whether the other person has a similar approach to self-discipline without first knowing just how self-disciplined you are. Or just how committed to self-development. Compatibility of priorities. Compatibility of outlook. Compatibility of worldview.

Compatibility, therefore, begins with us, with knowing ourselves. I cannot aspire to be with a man who is extremely disciplined about food, exercise and lifestyle without first assessing where I stand on this aspect of self-discipline. Too much of a gap can turn into a chasm. While we do not aspire to be with or marry our own twin, we need to be on a similar plane. More importantly, to know and understand what the other is all about. And whether these elements in the other are acceptable to us.

Self-development and self-discipline begin with the self'. In life and in learning, the other element of the self, aka motivation (self-motivation), plays a major role. The drive, the need to succeed, and the openness to learn are the foundations of that motivation. Staying the course is the next level.

Compatibility is about finding and nurturing relationships. Be it a mate, a partner, a friend or a companion. The Buddha taught that with the right skills and understanding, such a partnership can be one of happiness and satisfaction and form the basis of progress and prosperity.

The idea that happiness in life and in relationships is all about skills gives hope. Even the greatest skills can be learned. They can be acquired. Even mastered. This brings hope to someone in difficult circumstances. Hope to someone who is on the verge of giving up on their dreams. Hope to someone who may otherwise give up on finding a partner.

TO BE MARRIED HAPPILY...

A TIME OF MANY REALIZATIONS

'Love was my only reason to marry.
An integral or cardinal part of it.
I married only because of love.
I was an independent career woman.
My music and my career were priority for me.
Music defines my personality and my being.
I chose marriage based on friendship, love,
understanding and companionship.'

—Shibani Kashyap (in a personal chat)

Time flew by. On the wings of speed, hope, warmth and good old-fashioned lust. Milestones blinked past us. Within a month of meeting each other, we made the down payment on our first home together. Our engagement took place at the three-month mark. We shared the dream of a future together. We got down to the practical stuff: making arrangements and spending our earnings to build a life together.

An amazing feeling of freedom and happiness marked it all. Each moment was committed to memory. Framed in deep gratitude. Brushed with the rainbow hues of tenderness, romance and togetherness. There were movies beyond recall, with endless tubs of popcorn and somewhat corny hand-holding. Parties with friends, pubbing, watching the FIFA World Cup finals in a posh lounge. Cheering madly and grinning at each other through it all. There was also quiet time with each other.

A friendship was being forged—deep, interesting, pleasant and by mutual action. By mutual consent.

I wondered why more people didn't opt for a later marriage that allowed for full freedom. Freedom of choice, of time and of money. Freedom to focus completely. I wondered why more people did not wait until later to find someone special to share the fullness of their lives with.

I had been in love earlier, of course. I had fancied myself in love even more times than that. But this was different. The absolute sense of enjoyment and the complete freedom to plan. The freedom to be. The freedom to love. The freedom to be my own person and let him be his. To love and be loved. Without neediness. With strength and purpose. Our areas of collaboration were well defined. Workdays were defined and planned. The work of building a home and getting married was as exacting as it was exciting.

We had roped in my dad and Manu's mom into the whole enterprise of marriage, creating and building a new home, and setting up our independent establishment. We also kept them somewhat distanced from taking over and managing the whole thing. It was a textbook case of learning balance. A balance between our desires, our dreams and the responsibilities that we both had. A balance between time spent with each other even as we took care of our respective work, our lives and our parents.

It was a conscious effort to balance it all. To fulfil our duties and work on our desires. Perhaps this was what was meant in these lines from my much loved copy of *The Little Prince*: 'Love does not consist of gazing at each other, but in looking outward together in the same direction.'

We had taken on a huge home loan together. I had to face my dad's disapproval. He thought it madness that I had taken this on within such a short time of meeting Manu. I understood his concern and spoke with him about my conviction and our following the right course of action together. I am not sure I was able to convince him very much. The home loan was from a public-sector bank, which had put us through the hoops of documentation and due process. The bank was getting our home insured as well and did a comprehensive medical check on us. My results were not too shabby. All the exercising and eating right were paying off. For me, the incentive was looking fabulous on my wedding day and thereafter.

One day, Manu called to say that he was coming over to meet me for a chat. I thought it was strange, as he didn't usually specify things like that. We would meet for hours every weekend and a couple of evenings during the week, depending on our workload. Anyway, a tall glass of cold coffee was chilling in the fridge, and Prema, my cook, would make a couple of snacks.

He appeared relaxed, but I could sense that something was bothering him. What was he here to say? To chat about? 'What's up, Manu?' I asked, keeping the small kernel of worry firmly within.

'GP, you know that I lost my dad in 1996. He was a chain smoker and had developed a heart condition in his late 50s or early 60s. He was being careful and then died of a misdiagnosed heart attack. It was the turning point in my life and in our family.'

I wondered where this was going. The kernel of worry was unfurling and would soon bloom. I could feel the hard press of anxiety in my stomach. It was only my sincere practice of Gautam's guidance for the past seven years that kept me quiet with a modicum of calm. My strength of mind kept that hard press of anxiety at bay.

After a few moments, Manu continued, 'Our medical tests were comprehensive, and I know that you are happy with your results. As it should be. But my treadmill stress test shows that my heart skipped a couple of beats. The insurance physician says there is some problem, and I should get it checked out with a cardiologist.'

I was blindsided. What did this mean? What was this all about? Why was this happening? Why now? And why to me?

'Whoa!' Gautam's voice spoke in my heart. 'Is this about you?' Gautam seemed to be asking: 'This is about the person you claim to love and care about. Can you not see and understand it from his point of view? Can you not see and understand the stress he is experiencing?'

As Manu seemed steeped in his own thoughts, I took a few deep and calming breaths. Breathe in to the count of 6, hold to the count of 6 and breathe out to the count of 8. Slowly. With focus. I could feel the shift within my body and mind. The hard kernel of anxiety loosened its hold in just a few moments.

'So, Manu, what about it? I am not sure what you are saying.' My voice was now calm and gentle as I prompted him to share his thoughts.

His hesitation was visible as he said, 'I guess what I am trying to say is that if you want to reevaluate your decision to marry me given this finding . . .' he trailed off. Within moments, he had steeled himself to continue, 'I won't hold it against you. I will always love and respect you, no matter what you decide. No matter what you choose. But, GP, think about it with a cool mind and decide in your own best interest. I will always be there for you.'

Ah!

Was it in my late teens or early twenties that I read the fabulous love story of Nisha JamVwal and Kanwar Rameshwar Singh Jamwal? I still remember the tears that flowed as I read their story in Lord Jeffrey Archer's *And Thereby Hangs a Tale*. It moved me beyond expression and left me wishing that it had only been fiction and not fact.

Love is not always about moving from success to success nor does it always follow a straight path. Life is filled with the unexpected. Nisha and KRS had fallen deeply in love, fought through obstacles of time and distance, braved the displeasure of his royal family and remained true to their vows to each other. Only to face the stark tragedy of a massive accident within hours of marriage.

Nisha had stuck with her love and her vows. She camped that first year of her married life in the hospital, where they worked their way through the trauma, the shock and the enormity of the accident that had shaken their world in the prime of life and within hours of marriage.

Now, a million thoughts and emotions were ready to swamp me.

Manu's stress and concern were alive forces in the living room. His frankness and generosity of spirit were visible. I had known pain and suffering for the better part of my life. I was seeking certainty, and I was seeking my forever kind of companionship. Given my lived experiences, the answer was crystal clear.

Slowly, I sat up straighter. I took a few more moments of focused and calm breathing. A few moments to connect with my inner self. I did not want to react quickly and regret it at leisure. My words and my decision would echo through our lives. His and mine. For once, I would be clear and calm and choose the right course of action. I would choose what was right for me. In my interest. To my benefit. From my better vantage point in life.

My mind calm and my voice firm, I said slowly, 'Manu, I understand what you are saying and why you are saying it. I don't have words to express my appreciation of what you are saying and the choices you are offering me at this stage of our relationship.

'I absolutely agree that I should choose what is in my best interest. As you know, Gautam has been mentoring me on my journey through life over the last few years. I can literally feel his presence right here, and I can say with certainty that what I am saying to you is something he would agree with.

'The choice is so clear that there really is no choice in this matter. We need to move ahead in life. Together. It is a matter of chance that we applied for the home loan just a few months before getting married. Had we gotten married in May or June and then applied for the home loan, the result of the medical investigation for insurance would have come after marriage, wouldn't it? If this same thing had happened post-marriage, would you still be giving me this choice? Would there be any choice but to move forward as a couple? I know enough about life by now to know that there are no guarantees in life. There is no insurance policy that can spare us the uncertainty of life.

'Our relationship remains, and we will stay the course. It could very well be that my medical reports were not normal. What would you have done in that case?'

The silence spun and throbbed with emotion.

It was a while before Manu responded to my last question, 'Thank you, GP. My respect for you has gone up by leaps and bounds. I think you know very well that if the situation were reversed, my answer would have been the same. We stay together. We are together.'

The intent to stay together was at the heart of every decision. We were not second-guessing our decision about being right for each other. We were not considering whether there was someone better out there for us. We were not shopping for more options, better options or perfect options.

My heart was full. With love. With gratitude. With appreciation.

The stress of work had melted away, receding into the background. I had never felt better. Never looked better. Each element of life was blooming. I began to understand that life is a true mirror—not a reverse one. The gratitude, positivity and confidence I was experiencing and doubtless exuding helped life become and feel better than ever. And because life was good and better than ever, I was continuing to experience positivity at work and in other relationships. The inner feeling of buoyancy and positivity somehow helped others relate to me more positively. There was less friction and negativity at work.

The surge of confidence within brought about a sense of security and a feeling that I was in control. It allowed for calmness and composure within. I was making better professional decisions. And gaining more positivity and confidence from them. The effort to build a future and a home together meant a tremendous focus on goals. And the time crunch added an interesting dimension to it all. As did managing the emotions and sensitivities of our families. Manu's mom and sisters. My dad.

We were surely looking in the same direction, as we faced some similar challenges in managing our lives. And yet, there was an ease to doing it all. In managing it all. I recalled something that Gautam had shared with me: 'It is very important to be in love. To experience

> *Being in love with yourself is the most vital and important aspect of love.*

all that love brings. Begin with yourself. Being in love with yourself is the most vital and important aspect of love. Be grateful to be who you are. Appreciate yourself. Be kind to yourself when you make mistakes. Take care of yourself—after all, don't we always look after those whom we love? And we do it without holding back and without begrudging the effort, the work or the feeling of responsibility'.

How right and how wise . . . The energy wasted in doing things grudgingly and with complaint is what drains us. When we work with a sense of purpose, with clear goals in sight, energized by our love for ourselves, for our work and for others, it is magical. It brings out our best. We bring out life's best.

Another challenge lay ahead. Dad's medical issues were surfacing. He was stressed about my marriage and the fact that it meant I would leave home. And he would be alone. He was now 80 years old. The prospect of living alone, even though I would visit him every other day and the existing maids would continue to work for him, daunted him. He was sensitive about the fact that he was not really in the driver's seat, even though he was part of the discussions. I could sense his growing anxiety.

He was fine up until a month and a half before D-Day. But then he suddenly developed a health condition that required major surgery.

This was perhaps one more trial for me. To assess how much I had truly changed as a person. The timing of it was no coincidence. How would I deal with this? With disappointment and frustration? With resentment towards the whole matter and holding close questions of why me and why now? There was a direct impact on my fiercely protected leave from work. I had been scrounging and saving it all for the wedding and the post-wedding work and travel.

I considered giving in to the frustration that was trying to creep in. I considered picking up the phone and reaching out to Gautam. But I stopped myself.

This was perhaps not the time to seek more exercises and advice from him. It was a time to show how effective those exercises had been and how I had evolved as a person.

If I had truly changed, it would show in the way I related to the problem at hand. All the work I had been doing on myself these past seven years stood firm in the face of this obstacle. Dad's health and situation were important, and I would simply have to make the time to get it done. I was grateful to have Manu by my side at this time. And my prayers were deep. I needed my father to be truly well, happy and mobile by the time of our wedding on 2 October.

Help flowed my way in the form of close doctor friends. The surgery was expensive, as I chose to get it done in a private hospital under the overall supervision of my doctor friend. My priorities were clear. I would choose the more expensive option over the lesser cost of a government hospital, as I wanted the best care for my dad.

This shift within me started showing startling results outside. I stumbled on my mother's old files, which I had lost sight of. They contained share certificates, the value of which would easily cover my wedding expenses and more. I was steeped in gratitude. It seemed she was still looking out for me. Gautam's words echoed within: 'Love and gratitude bring us grace from the universe. It flows outward from us. Gratitude is perhaps the only thing that mellows the hard edge of our lives and our karma, and allows us to create a better life.'

Breakthroughs in life, changing the pattern of hardship in relationships, overcoming challenges—everything boils down to gratitude and living with clear priorities.

'As Buddhahood arises from within, it finds protection from without.'

—Nichiren Daishonin,
thirteenth-century Japanese sage

... AND TO BE HAPPILY MARRIED

A CONTINUED STRUGGLE FOR HAPPINESS

'My lay followers develop confidence in
their spiritual path, discipline themselves,
acquire more knowledge, practice generosity
and gain wisdom.'

—The Buddha (*The Numerical Discourses*)

I was revelling in the new, the glorious rush and the sheer headiness of it all—finding my partner, our new home and our new life together. The decisions and choices I had made.

I thought and believed that I had left behind the old. This was a fresh start. A new phase of life. One where I would not be disturbed by the old. Old problems, old concerns and old troubles. Now that I was married, life would be simply perfect.

Now that I was married, life was . . . how shall I put it? Life was simply **not** perfect. We had rented an apartment a few floors below Manu's, where my mother-in-law and two sisters-in-law lived. We began married life on a very simple and austere note. Manu refused to do up our rented apartment because it was a stop-gap measure. We were waiting to take possession of our new home, and we would do **that** up, not this one.

I was back at work and working long and hard hours. Life was even more complex. I had to look out for Dad and watch out for the sensibilities and sensitivities of my in-laws. Things were not always cordial, despite my desire to be a part of the new family. I was not getting the response

I had truly hoped for. My sisters-in-law kept to themselves. With four of her own daughters, my mother-in-law candidly told me that she was not looking to add one more. She did promise to be my friend. And until the end of her life, she was friendly and cordial. Yet, my longing for a mother's love and affection and the intense need to be accepted, embraced with warmth and become a part of a large family were not finding fulfilment.

Everything was different. The way of life itself had changed. With the additional physical and emotional demands on me, my stress was rising. My well-trained house staff had made my life and my working hours so much easier. But they were left behind with Dad. A few miles away. I had to fend for myself.

Adding to my woes were physical pain and discomfort. I fractured two toes on my left foot while running on the hard sand on my honeymoon. It had happened in a split second before the parasailing rope tugged me up several miles above the deep sea. I clung to the rope, shivering with my fears of water and height. Sobbing with pain and fear. Hoping that I would live long enough to kill Manu, who had been responsible for my hard fall on the hard-packed sand. He had distracted me just as I was running before being towed up.

Day four of the honeymoon went by in the hospital, where I got my foot X-rayed and strapped. Buying new footwear that would allow the swollen, strapped foot to ease in. Limping all the way back. Just limping with pain. Some honeymoon, I muttered to myself. Manu's tenderness towards me saved his life many times over the next few days. The ribbing and jokes I faced once back at work nearly made me turn murderer. Manu was just lucky that I had better impulse control thanks to Gautam's exercises, I thought to myself!

Gautam had been right. Marriage was no sanctuary against life. No sanctuary against the problems of life. It had brought some new ones in. The unsettled feeling continued.

Was the possession of the new home now going to be the next mirage I would chase in my attempt to settle down? What would happen?

The sheer volume of work was stressful in itself. Businesses were growing, and new products were being added at the India Today Group. The turnaround time for new hires was a killer. I was doing my best but was limited by the feeling of not being in the driver's seat of my life. At home, Manoj was performing a tightrope act—balancing relationships, his time and his attention. He was managing his stress much better than I was managing mine. Until our exchange of words spiralled and I told him that I would not return home.

It was with trepidation that I drove to my dad's place in the evening after work. I let myself in with my keys. Dad was watching TV and was really happy to see me. I warmed up the leftovers in the fridge and ate them while sitting with my dad. We chatted for a bit, and then dad said he wanted to sleep. He asked me to leave. I said I was staying the night. He frowned and asked me if all was well. 'I am just sorting out a few things,' I answered. 'Well, you need to do that at your home,' pat came Dad's response. He was not going to let me stay for the night. Gently but firmly, he asked me to go back.

Reluctantly, I drove through the gathering shadows of the oncoming night. Manu was delighted to see me. The smile on his face was tender and beautiful. I would not be easy to pacify, I told myself.

Manu played squash every evening. It was the secret behind his lean and fit physique. As the evening advanced, I could see his post-game and end-of-day fatigue, and soon he excused himself and went to bed. Sulking and lost in my misery, I refused to give him the satisfaction of turning in at the same time. I was determined to drag it out despite my own tiredness and the hard, long day that awaited me in the office the following morning.

I sat in our sparsely furnished living area. It only consisted of a trio of chairs. The armchairs had been carted over in the car from my dad's place. With Manu stuck on his no-waste, no unnecessary expense mantra, we were only making do with basic stuff and whatever was strictly necessary. We were some months away from receiving possession of our new home. How many months? It was anyone's guess. That evening, I started browsing through the latest stack of magazines that I had carried home from work the previous few days. I had loved magazines since I was a child, growing up on a steady diet of them. It was an indulgence and not just a part of my work. Something I truly enjoyed and looked forward to.

In the stack was the glossy and most recent issue of the newly launched *Men's Health*. The cover sure caught my eye! I was flicking through the pages when I came to an interview with the tycoon Yash Birla. His interview was interesting. He seemed to be an unusual man, and even more so, an unusual industrialist. Buff and fit. Clearly, fitness was his religion. And yet, he had a depth of understanding that shone through in his responses to the questions posed to him in the interview. A line from his interview leaped straight out at me. 'Marriage is an experience for spiritual growth.'

> *Marriage is an experience for spiritual growth.*

The line seemed to sear itself into my eyes and my mind. *Marriage is an experience for spiritual growth.* What did he mean by that? I now needed to understand this in greater detail. It would have to wait until the morning as wave after wave of fatigue lapped at me. There was no way I could bunk down on the armchair for the remaining hours of the night. My body was cramped and stiff. I needed to stretch out until the alarm rang in the morning.

The need for sleep was urgent. The need to understand marriage was even greater. The morning would come soon enough. One need could be managed in the present; the other would have to wait.

'Most people have not tapped into nor understood their own rhythm let alone have the capacity to flow into or with another's rhythm.'

—Gautam (in a personal chat)

GAUTAM'S GUIDANCE

Gautam said to me, 'GP, hold on to what I am telling you today. It is at the heart of marriage. Of all human relationships. You have to start to understand that all relationships are demanding. They demand mindfulness, acknowledgement and effort. Relationships are equally about the other person and us. Not the other alone. Not us alone. But both. In equal measure.

'Mr Yash Birla's understanding of marriage is profound. What does spirituality really mean? It does not mean ritual or worship of something or someone. It means living life well and trying to bring our best to the game of life. What does living life well mean? Living well means being wholesome, progressive and focused on what is important to you as an individual. It means being responsible and committed to yourself, and then whatever you say is important to you. It means contributing to the people around you, starting with those immediately in front of you—your spouse, your partner, your children, your parents and your siblings.

'From there, you receive training on how to be and how not to be with friends, extended family, colleagues and bosses. Eventually, with society. And the ripples spin out to encompass the world. Just like having a sibling alters our ability to care and share, having a partner or spouse is about expanding our ability to care and share. In many ways, a partnership or marriage is like a friendship with benefits. But it's not limited to occasional sex. It is about having someone to chat with, interact with, share with and walk the path of life with. It is about contributing to the larger cause—of society, of social wealth, even of training the next generation. It involves contributing to another's life in positive ways.

'Courtship is exciting because it brings out our best. We learn that we have the capacity to love another person. The other person arouses and engages our ability to love. They may or may not be loveable, but our ability and capacity to love them is engaged. Our capacity to love is always within us. It just needs the right catalyst to peep out and transform our lives for those days and months. So meeting that special someone is the catalyst to bring out the wonderful rush of feelings, emotions and hormones. The ones that make life so amazing and wonderful.

'No effort is too much during courtship. Charged with tremendous energy, we have the ability to move mountains—at least we feel like that. We enjoy and eagerly look forward to pleasing our partner. Doing stuff for them. With them. Our pleasure at hearing from them is undimmed, even on the fifth phone call of the day. We celebrate the smallest of milestones—the anniversary of the first date, the first month and whatever else. We celebrate having someone in our lives. Because that person is bringing out our best. Making me a better me.

'The truth is that relationships are hard work. Everyone knows and accepts that parenting is tremendous work. Yet, somehow, understanding does not extend to romantic and sexual relationships. Certainly not to marriage. It is not effortless. Romance takes effort. Dating takes effort. A fit body is about the effort that goes into it. A loving relationship between adults, particularly a long-term partnership, requires a tremendous amount of work.

'Over time, as we become used to the catalyst of the wonderful, our feelings become muted. We begin to get less and less excited about the whole thing. The magic is no longer magical. So what has changed? The love and the capacity to love are still within us. We created the magic that we experienced because someone stirred us. The question is not what lifted the magic spell but what we can do to make the sparkling, effervescent feelings last.'

'What indeed?' I wondered what could be the key to unlocking that magic spell and keeping it alive. I was ready with my recorder and my fat notebook. There was work coming up for me. Work on myself as a person. Work on the relationship with Manu to keep the magic alive. I was realizing quickly that it was not just about getting married happily but rather about being happily married.

Gautam gave me the following points to reflect on and work on:

1. Love yourself. Work on yourself. You are the biggest work in progress in your own life. Work really hard on yourself.
2. Manage the stress of the other parts of your life. This will ensure that it remains contained and does not rub off on the relationship.
3. Acknowledge and appreciate each other. Always. It will help you experience the magic again and again.
4. Continue to celebrate the ordinary. Make date night your ritual in the quest to experience the magic. Be flexible and spontaneous about the timing and nature of the date. But jealously

guard this time. It is the key to making the magic spell last.

5. Spend time away from each other. Be it for work, for a project or for travel that you have always wanted to do. A solo vacation. A vacation with friends and buddies. A college reunion. Whatever. Don't insist on always doing things together. Do it on your own. And allow the other to do it as well.

'I used to bring flowers for Gauri (Gauri Pradhan) every single day. Every evening. I have done this for years. It was important for me to do this. Not just a gesture. I used to select the flowers myself and see her delight. Now, I bring flowers for Gauri every week. Not because we've been married for nineteen years but because our house would be filled with flowers and they were getting spoiled (since I was bringing them every day). It gives me such pleasure to do this for Gauri.'

—Hiten Tejwani (in a personal chat)

THE BUDDHA'S WORDS
OF WISDOM

'When both partners trust each other, **use pleasant words**
To communicate with each other, have
self-discipline and maintain
Upright conduct, their progress increases and
pleasant life is born!'
—The Buddha (*The Numerical Discourses*)

The Buddha taught his followers the basics of successful relationships and how to nurture them. A clear understanding, focus and intent are at the heart of successful and happy relationships. According to the teachings of the Buddha, both the masculine and the feminine have specific roles. He explained that it was essential for **both** partners to play their roles for mutual benefit and satisfaction.

FOR HIM

Interestingly, the Buddha's instructions to men precede his instructions to women.

1. Respect and Admiration for Women

The Pali term *sammananaya* includes respect, admiration and refraining from disrespect. Another interpretation is 'with honour'. The importance that the Buddha accorded to this above all else is clearly visible—everything that follows is either secondary or flows from this element of respect and honour.

Modern life bears witness to the disharmony that results from not honouring our partners. Be they our life partners, romantic partners or even our business partners. Separation after separation, divorce after divorce, fight after fight—almost all stem from the feeling of not being respected and honoured. A key aspect of being respected is having the freedom to be, to do, to say and to be heard. Respect is tangible and visible in our words and in our actions towards others.

The Buddha referred to marriage as a partnership. Partnerships work on free will and choice. Partnerships work with equality, fair play and mutual respect. We enter into partnerships out of our own free will. We treat the other person as an equal. This is the intent of the Buddha—to treat the feminine, the woman, as an equal. Treat her with respect and honour. Appreciate her.

2. Choosing Words Wisely, Mindfully

Choosing words wisely is not about being wise and knowledgeable in speech. It is not about posturing. It is simply about refraining from doing what is hurtful or disrespectful. It is about refraining from unpleasant speech.

Harsh and unpleasant speech is never helpful in any relationship. The Buddha spoke of the necessity of pleasant and respectful speech in many different contexts. Harsh speech never solves problems nor brings people closer.

Yet, stopping a hot rejoinder or cutting remark is difficult without being mindful. And without the underpinning of respect.

3. Fidelity and Remaining Faithful

The Buddha asked husbands to first be mindful of their own faithfulness before enquiring into their wife's loyalty. He discouraged extramarital relationships for all his followers, both men and women. While acknowledging impulsive sexual urges as a powerful and insistent force, the Buddha instructed his followers to be mindful and refrain from sexual misconduct. Fidelity and faithfulness bloom from respect and appreciation for the woman and the family.

4.   Give Up Authority and Dominance

Dominance and authority stop harmony and are against the spirit of respect and equality in any partnership, especially the marital partnership. The Buddha candidly asked men to give up dominating behaviour for the sake of harmony and success in marriage.

He asked women not to assume a doormat's role in any relationship but to step up and take an equal role in decision-making, taking responsibility and being progressive.

5.   Gifts and Generosity

The Buddha asked men to be generous in the giving of gifts and ornaments. The Pali term *alankara anuppadana* translates to adornments and gifts. A different translation of the same, in the *Sigalovada Sutra*, refers to it as ornaments of gold, silver and pearls. Essentially, it means generosity. The giving and sharing of prosperity. An understanding that women like and appreciate beauty and the beautiful. And that sometimes the tangible is a reminder of being valued in a relationship. Though it is not a measure of value, it is a visible reminder and valuable for that.

Thus the woman, the feminine, will feel connected to her male partner and, in turn, the relationship will be happy and harmonious.

For Her

The wife, too, has a distinct role to play. The Buddha enjoined on her the following duties.

1. Work in an Organized Way

The home needs to be well organized and to work well for success and progress outside of it.

In Pali, the term used for women performing their duties is *susanvihita kammanta hoti*. The Buddha didn't refer to chores at home. Only the organization of work. He encouraged women to be well organized, irrespective of the nature of their work. This, perhaps, was also an acknowledgement of the different hats that women wear and their multitasking.

The Buddha never confined women to home and hearth. He was an unequivocal champion and advocate for women and their voice, their freedom and rights. He placed them as equals on the intellectual plane.

So, this exhortation is **not** about the kind of work but rather about the way of working. Whatever a woman's occupation, the Buddha encouraged her to be organized with her work.

2. Managing the Retinue (Around the Household)

In the Buddha's social context, the retinue encompassed family members, friends and employees. This instruction refers to the interpersonal management of those relationships. Even though social roles have evolved and changed with time, this exhortation seems relevant even now.

3. Fidelity and Being Faithful

Not just husbands, but wives are asked to be faithful too. Being faithful means refraining from sexual misconduct, which applies equally to men and women.

4. Protecting Wealth and Provisions

Balance was the key to the Buddha's teachings. He urged the use of wealth and all resources with moderation, neither being stingy nor spendthrift. To quote from Bhikkhu Basnagoda Rahula on this aspect of the Buddha's teachings: '(a wife) should not swindle, save greedily or waste away the wealth, but protect it'.

This approach to family fortunes and resources is one that is bound to increase trust and win the respect of the other partner. A win-win proposition.

5. Skill and Energy

Whether the duty is solely managing home, hearth and children or juggling roles that cut across studying and writing, a professional identity **and** still managing home, hearth and children, women are always tasked with a lot. In all that she does and wants to do, the Buddha asks her to show skill and energy.

6. Role as Companion and Guide

A woman need not be a follower. She is an entity in her own right. Her contribution to a relationship goes beyond any social expectation or context. This instruction from the Buddha acknowledges this. A companion is a friend and an equal. A guide has the other person's best interests at heart and speaks up to say their bit when needed.

Successful collaborations and partnerships need equal contributions, participation and work by all the parties involved. Harmony in cohabiting, harmony in sharing personal space, harmony in sharing a life, harmony in marriage—all are delicate affairs. A balance is needed to make it strong, robust and enjoyable for those in it. It is not about enforcing rights or complaining about what is lacking, but rather about loving give and take. For a mutually rewarding relationship, both parties must understand what is needed to progress and do what is necessary with the right attitude.

'It is the power of the bow that determines the flight of the arrow, the might of the dragon that controls the movement of the clouds and the strength of the wife that guides the actions of her husband.'

—Nichiren Daishonin,
thirteenth-century Japanese sage

IN THE DRIVER'S SEAT
A DEEPER UNDERSTANDING OF COMMITMENT

commitment
noun
a promise to do or give something
a promise to be loyal to someone or something
the attitude of someone who works very hard to do or
support something
being prepared to give a lot of your time and attention to
something because you believe it is right or important
a promise or agreement to do something; a responsibility

Life was busy, busy, busy, almost like it was on steroids. So much was happening between work, writing, Manu and all our other responsibilities. Those towards our surviving parents—his mother and my dad. Towards our siblings. Taking care of multiple homes and taking care of so much. We had also become parents over the last few years, blessed to have our two girls. And yes, the workload had increased and the multiple roles were demanding. There was stress and there was a sense of tiredness. It was not easy being the caregiver to multiple generations with the added complexity of siblings who needed to be looked after on both sides. And we weren't exactly spring chickens ourselves.

It was sheer chance that I spotted Gautam's message. He was inviting me to an uber-luxury retreat overseas. The retreat was scheduled to start after a week. My stay and travel were being taken care of. I was being invited to chronicle the retreat and publish a white paper on the discussions that would unfold under Gautam's tutelage. This was the first in a series planned by the portal.

Gautam's message was just the thing. I always tried to honour his guidance and have the occasional couple of days by myself. Manu travelled solo more frequently. For work, to be with his friends, for his school reunions and much more. Travelling solo meant that one of us was around the girls and all the people who needed our care and attention. Travelling on our own was easier on the mind and much less stressful because the other person was managing the home base. Besides, the warmth and sizzle of the homecoming were always the highlights!

The journey with Gautam was an experience in itself. He was feted and wooed on the airline and when we reached the island resort. Clearly, I was travelling in august company! Gautam continued to be his calm and pleasant self. His briefing to me on the flight out was clear. He had been invited by the portal to host the long weekend. It was a unique concept. The weekend would consist of couples that were intending to marry and three that had been married a long time. There were also single folk, seeking help in finding and learning how to build a relationship. The to-be-married had questions, perhaps concerns, about the relationship they were embarking upon, and the three married couples were there to chat about their journey. Or maybe they were trying to recapture the magic of love.

It was not a training programme or a workshop, but a unique concept—a series of transformative discussions and conversations with their clients. I was the scribe and moderator. I needed to create icebreakers and get the ball rolling. Keep the conversation alive and move it to the next level. The portal was keen to publish a white paper on it. The whole idea was to create a record, a legacy of the interaction with Gautam, and help others in the future. They wanted to create a series of these transformative conversations.

Sparkling blue water surrounded our resort. We were in a place of stunning beauty. Clearly, the hosting portal had pulled out all the stops. We scattered to our rooms with a clear agenda to meet in the pavilion reserved for us and our conversation.

When we regrouped in the pavilion, we were all carrying the look and the cool vibe of the islands—colourful cottons, pastels in linen, printed cool shirts, skirts and a few shorts, invariably sandals. There was an inviting spread of tropical fresh fruit, sandwiches, baked yogurt and cookies. Tea, coffee, sparkling and still water competed for space on the long tables at the front of the pavilion. There was the usual melee for food and a bit of self-conscious catch-up.

I had to settle down towards the head of the long table. But before I could do that, I quickly counted off all the participants. Gautam and myself, and the two reps from the company. We were a group of eighteen people, along with the three married couples and the rest of the portal users. Not everyone was from India. Some of the folks had flown in from different parts of the world. Moving from group to group and individual to individual, I asked everyone to come to the table and settle down. With some cajoling and some prompting, we were soon all seated around the table.

Before the trip, the portal had worked out an outline for the three-day retreat. Gautam had asked me to get involved in it. He did not like very rigid agendas and always allowed room for conversations to evolve. I thought hard. After some research, I recommended to them that we start by looking at the three elements of the triangular theory of love developed by psychologist Robert Sternberg. He presented the idea that the three components of love are intimacy, passion and commitment. We would kickstart the retreat within this broad framework. And, of course, discussions and conversations would naturally evolve from there. Everyone could share their thoughts and even ask questions.

The first discussion in the series was on commitment. I was looking forward to a robust dialogue, even as a part of me wondered if everyone would be on the same page. I was also a bit nervous since the topic sounded heavy. I was keen and curious to understand commitment better, and could only hope that others were too. Gautam brought his own unique insight to everything. His wisdom and style were both inimitable. And here, he was the main draw. The main lynchpin holding it all together.

Introductions had already been made. I eased into an icebreaker and followed it up with an expectation-setting session so that expectations were out in the open. What is commitment, after all, and why were we gathered here to explore it and understand it better? What did everyone expect from today's conversation?

Everyone rushed in to share their point of view on commitment. A few smart ones were quickly trying to see the definition on their smart-er phones. Riya from the portal was noting the individual definitions on a large flip chart, one of two in the pavilion. It became clear rather quickly that everyone was interested in understanding commitment and what it would mean in their married lives in the times and years ahead.

The initial rush gave way to a gap of silence. Something was off-kilter with at least one of the three married couples. The note of bitterness in Meena's voice was unmistakable when she said, 'Oh, commitment.' Within the next minute she sharply thrust her chair back and turned to walk away to the end of the pavilion. Something had to be done. And quickly. I decided to jump in and asked Sumit, her husband: 'Sumit, you and Meena have been married for several years now. How do you read the definition of commitment in your life?'

The tall and muscular Sumit looked fleetingly at Meena, his wife of nineteen years, and said, 'Whenever I think of commitment, I think it is about being around and fulfilling my duties to the family.'

There were visible signs of irritation in Meena's body language. Would she have the courage to speak up about what was bothering her? Or would I have to prompt her in anyway? My thoughts were interrupted by Meena's comment, 'As you know, Sumit and I have been married for nineteen years. Sumit makes medical and surgical equipment. I was previously the marketing head of a large multinational company. But I have taken some time out for myself. Taken a break. I don't know about the psychology of love, but I am here to find some answers to my problems with Sumit.'

Meena's tone was crisp and somewhat angry. Beneath the anger lay an undertone of hurt and confusion. I was instantly sympathetic and asked, 'Do go on and share something about the answers you are seeking. Perhaps you both are seeking, then.'

'Meena . . .' Sumit pleaded in a whisper.

'I know Sumit does not want me to say this. But we are here to try to save our marriage. Sumit cheated on me. Cheated on our marriage. With my cousin. Were it not for my 17-year-old son and 15-year-old daughter, we would not be here. I would have divorced him and taken him to the cleaners.' Her tone was fierce. I could see what it had cost her. Her nails dug into the palms of her hands, leaving a deep impression. 'My cousin is divorced and single. Sumit has apologized to me and asked me to give him another chance. I am working to get over the sense of betrayal and hurt. But I just feel so let down. Even now, I regret agreeing to a second chance. I just hope that whatever unfolds in the next few days here will help me put this behind me. Will help me heal and move forward in life. With or without marriage.'

The silence was brittle. Gazes averted and slid away from Meena and Sumit. They finally rested on Gautam. The expectation was clear. He was here to help and find solutions to all that we had experienced and would experience.

There was a wealth of understanding and compassion in Gautam's eyes, and his voice was oh-so gentle and kind as he said, 'Thank you, Meena, for sharing what you have. It is always so difficult to be this candid and frank. Thank you, Sumit, for being here and for having the strength to want to change. Your presence means a lot to me personally and to all of us.

'The sexual impulse is not easy to tame. It is one of the strongest forces within human beings. And modern life brings plenty of sexual stimulus even as it does away with true desire. Yet, taming sexual impulses is the key to true intimacy and a deeper sense of connectedness.

'Meena, you say that you would have left Sumit but for your children. I fully appreciate the necessity of staying together for the sake of your young kids. They are both at a sensitive stage of life. But perhaps this reason alone is not enough for you and Sumit to stay together. An unhappy marriage or forced relationship is not the right environment in which to raise children, whatever their age. They absorb the intense negativity of their environment, however well you both believe you are playing the part of everything being normal and as per usual.'

Tears flooded Meena's eyes and began trickling down. Their soft plops were like a resounding echo in the now-silent space. 'Gautam, it is not only for the children's sake. There are so many factors. Our lives are so intertwined. Our finances, properties and investments over the last so many years. My mother and Sumit's father are both old and ailing. Our separation will be a shock to them as well. Nothing is simple after so many years. What is the right reasoning in this situation? I am still confused about what to do!'

Gautam took a moment before responding to Meena's heartfelt question, 'Children, parents, finances or even society and the complexity of a much intertwined life are not the right reasons to stay together. Stay with Sumit only if you are willing and able to start over. Only if you are willing to give him this second chance and a clean slate. His actions and choices are the cause of deep hurt and betrayal. It is not easy. His actions and choices have placed both of you in a state of misery and practical inconvenience and had a lasting impact, isn't it? Sumit, is this crossroad not inconvenient for you as well? How are you holding up?'

There was a depth of misery and suffering in Sumit's voice and words. Emotion had clogged his voice as well, and raggedly, he said, 'I honestly and a thousand times over regret what I did. There is simply no excuse for my mistake. I accept the fact that I cheated on our marriage. I let Meena down. I cheated on Meena with someone who is her cousin but is very much a part of the family and like a sister to Meena. I am aware that I have inflicted a double whammy on Meena. I have let her down. Heck, I have let myself down. There are days when I cannot bear to look at myself in the mirror.'

Sumit's anguish was a palpable force in the room. All movement and sound had ceased long ago.

After blowing his nose long and hard, Sumit turned to Gautam and continued, 'Gautam sir, you ask about the inconvenience. Let me tell you, the whole episode was inconvenient. Inconvenient in every way, and the fallout from it even more so. I know our daughter, Suhana, is aware of some of the facts. She has stopped interacting with me, and she is the apple of my eye. I love both my children, but I simply adore my daughter. My mother-in-law now hates me. My mistake has impacted my work and my productivity. I feel I have lost something significant within myself. If only I could undo what I have done . . . if only I could turn back the clock on the whole mess.'

Gautam was not unmoved by Sumit's anguish: 'Yes, Sumit. If only you could turn back the clock, and if only life permitted us to undo such life-changing mistakes. But in the absence of this, what do you propose to do? How do you propose to understand what led to this? How do both of you intend to move forward in life? For the rest of your lives?'

'I truly don't know, Gautam. I am at a loss for what to do. It has been four long months since the end of Sumit's relationship with my cousin. We signed up to be here as soon as a friend of ours told us about you and this workshop. The way forward is not clear to us. We were hoping . . .' Meena's voice trailed off, and she choked on her tears. Her self-restraint was truly heroic as she resumed, 'I am hoping to find some peace and understanding here. Some solutions from you.'

I could sense Gautam choosing his thoughts and words. Oh, he was never careless. Yet the sensitivity of the discussion, the raw emotions of Meena and Sumit, and the impact on everyone present were on another level. Our audience not only had couples who had been together for some time; it also included two engaged couples who were considering this retreat to be a sort of training ground for their forthcoming marriages.

Others were looking to understand marriage through these few days and were hopeful that the portal's proven algorithms and databases would support them in finding their right partners. The singles among the participants were not seeking to hook up or date endlessly but were keen on finding a life partner. More power to them, I thought. They were doing the right thing by preparing themselves for the next stage of life and understanding the right reasons to get married.

Gautam said, 'Would you mind sharing with us your reasons for entering into the relationship, Sumit? Why did you do it? What started it, and what caused it to end? As painful as these reflections can be for Meena and for you, it will be helpful to overcome the suffering and move forward. This understanding of your inner self is necessary if you truly wish to make a fresh start in life and in your relationships.'

Sumit took a long sip from his glass of water. Despite the lovely breeze and the four fans doing their work rather well, sweat gleamed on Sumit's face. He said slowly, 'Meena's cousin is often over at our place. She has been through a rough patch, and I was aware of it. With her marriage breaking down, she has had to struggle through life as a single parent. Initially, I was sympathetic to her plight. Especially since I was aware of the physical abuse in her relationship with her ex-husband. I tipped over from sympathy to something else when we found ourselves unexpectedly in Bangalore on work at the same time. It was madness. If only . . .'

Gautam, 'You felt sorry for Meena's cousin, but did you stop to think about Meena? Did you pause to think of the impact on your wife and your relationships at home? I am guessing not. Mistakes occur when we move mindlessly through life. It is like a terrible accident on a highway because we are not paying attention to oncoming traffic or the braking distance. We are not paying attention to the small child chasing the ball across the road. We are self-absorbed and even distracted. Distracted by the ringing phone. Distracted by our own thoughts. Distracted by the fight in the morning. Distracted by handsfree not connecting at the right time. Distracted, period. Inattentive, period. Unthinking, period. Mindless, period.

'It is vital to understand that being distracted, inattentive, unthinking and mindless is always the cause of accidents. It will always cause hurt and damage. So becoming mindful is the only solution. Stay mindful through your relationship and through life. Understand, know and accept that your life is always intertwined with others. Your actions are not in isolation. Each element impacts so many others.

'It is vital to understand that being distracted, inattentive, unthinking and mindless is always the cause of accidents. It will always cause hurt and damage. So becoming mindful is the only solution. Stay mindful through your relationship and through life. Understand, know and accept that your life is always intertwined with others. Your actions are not in isolation. Each element impacts so many others.

'Sumit, the hurt you have inflicted on your family is real and deep. You have taken something beautiful and crushed it. A crushed flower does not bloom again. And if you are not watchful and mindful, you can make a similar mistake again because opportunity and temptation exist all around us. Don't hold on to Meena simply because it is more convenient. If you want to choose a different life with a different set of values and actions, now is a good time.

'But please know that each time you aren't mindful, you damage yourself irreparably. You will be like the alcoholic who keeps falling off the wagon. The biggest commitment in life is to ourselves. To keep happy and healthy. To progress. To create value for ourselves and others. And to create value for the world and society. Falling off the wagon serves no purpose insofar as value creation or progress are concerned. Which means it directly impacts us and robs us of our happiness.

> *The biggest commitment in life is to ourselves. To keep happy and healthy. To progress. To create value for ourselves and others. And to create value for the world and society.*

'Commitment is a choice. It depends entirely on your free will.

'Each choice has consequences. Be aware of those. And I hope you will choose wisely.

'Meena, moving ahead with Sumit while holding on to this hurt is going to be impossible. The only way forward is to accept Sumit's apology and his regret and start afresh. If you keep holding this incident to the light every time you both have an argument or fight over something, then this is not going to work.

'And remember, a lot of it comes down to you. You are going to bump into your cousin at family get-togethers. Your children interact with hers. There is no way of avoiding her altogether. The onus is on you and you alone to erase this from your heart and start over with Sumit. To truly forgive.

And not blame them or even yourself continuously. If you make the choice to continue your marriage with Sumit and keep your family intact, you will need to overcome your anger and your pain. Your bitterness. Your blame.'

Gautam's voice carried power and conviction. His words rang true. Everyone was rapt. The words and advice clearly impacted both Sumit and Meena. They were sitting up straighter in their chairs, absorbing it all. Meena asked, more calmly than earlier, 'But is it not natural to be experiencing all this, Gautam? Am I wrong in any way?'

I was focused for the moment on a small byplay that went unnoticed by anyone else. Sumit reached for Meena's hand, and she drew hers back.

Gautam said, 'No, Meena. You are not wrong. Whatever you are experiencing is natural. The hurt and betrayal have wounded you deeply. All I am saying is that you need to leave these feelings behind, justified though they are. Whether you choose to stay with Sumit or not, you need to feel happy and at ease with the life ahead. These emotions are natural. But holding on to them will not be in your best interests. You are going to be continually reliving the hurt and the pain. Don't inflict that on yourself. Move forward and move ahead.

'Your biggest commitment is to yourself and working on your health and happiness. Only then will you be able to support your mother, your son and your daughter in the best way possible. If you are bitter, your children will suffer from that bitterness. If you are angry and hostile, your health will suffer. So whatever the decision, you have to strongly and deeply work on healing from within and putting this incident behind you.

'Sumit is in the wrong. What he did was unacceptable. **You** don't need to keep paying the price for Sumit's mistake. Your life is more precious than that.

'Marriage, or any exclusive relationship, is a choice. A choice to commit. To remain committed. If you are unable to make that commitment, then don't make the choice. But when you make the choice, honour yourself by keeping the commitment.

Marriage, or any exclusive relationship, is a choice. A choice to commit. To remain committed. If you are unable to make that commitment, then don't make the choice. But when you make the choice, honour yourself by keeping the commitment.

'A commitment goes beyond that of sexual or physical fidelity. It encompasses emotional and financial fidelity too. In today's world, it is also about bringing your wholehearted attention to the other person—not allowing gaming, snooker, friends, the best streaming platform, or whatever else to consume you. To learn to balance it all.

'In the 2009 film *Wanted*, when Salman Khan's character says, "*Ek baar jo maine commitment kar di, toh fir main apne aap ki bhi nahi sunta*" (Once I've made a commitment, I don't change it for anything. Not even when I tell myself differently), he is actually sharing a very profound truth. You must not listen to the voice of temptation or carelessness within. It is important not to give in to your temptations.

'There is a constant stream of sexual stimuli around us—ads, books, movies and adult content in different forms. Sex is a big part of life, but sex is not life, nor is life about sex. Physical attraction and chemistry matter a lot in a relationship, but commitment is a choice.

'People need to lead lives of greater awareness. Awareness of life and its governing principles. People may have different orientations, which is a part of life. Whether straight, gay or in any other form of relationship. It is a relationship with another human being that is pivotal to our own growth. True growth is about staying the course and experiencing the varied ups and downs of life.'

Vikram was an up-and-coming TV star. It was interesting to find him as one of the participants in the programme. His baritone was well known to anyone who watched TV. I nearly held my breath as he asked Gautam, 'So, Gautam, do you think there should be no separation at all or are you saying that divorce is somehow morally wrong?'

Gautam stood tall, his presence as powerful as ever. He was not fazed by whatever was coming his way. His deep understanding of relationships and human nature had made him an outstanding choice for this interesting get-away. He said, 'No, Vikram, I am not saying that at all. There are many reasons for separation. It is a matter of choice. Of free will. Where there is physical or mental abuse, your commitment to your own happiness should make you leave and not put up with it. But where there is no abuse, rushing to separate and divorce is not likely to bring happiness. Walking out of a relationship is no guarantee of happiness in the next one. Let's say for reasons of someone not making enough money, being difficult to live with, snoring, not allowing you enough social-media time, not supporting some of your choices or suddenly not being the person you thought you were marrying.

'The decision to separate and divorce cannot be taken lightly or for the wrong reasons. Both marriage and divorce require the right reasons and the right decision-making for them to succeed.

'There **is** one definition of commitment that is not up there on the flip chart. I rather like it—commitment in a relationship means you will keep treating your partner with respect, no matter what.'

The light breeze off the sea ruffled our hair and moved sinuously over the pavilion. A light dance of the sublime. The sound of water was just a hum in the background. Soothing and calm. It was time for a break.

MARA, THE TEMPTATION AND THE TEMPEST

Gautama, the renunciant, regained consciousness after fainting from near-starvation and resolved not to torture himself anymore with extreme practices. Bathing in the Niranjana River, he accepted the offering of thin rice gruel from Sujata, the daughter of the village headman.

He was now determined to attain enlightenment. He had prepared his body by accepting the nourishment of the gruel, and recovered by taking a soothing dip in the river water. His mind was clear, calm and focused on his goal.

Mara, the manipulator and distractor, appeared and engaged Gautama in a dialogue. Mara told Gautama that the Sakya kingdom was under immediate threat of being lost to the Sakya clan, and if Gautama left for Kapilavastu, the capital of the Sakya kingdom, he would be in time to save the kingdom. He would within a very short time become the *chakravartin raja*, or the great monarch that destiny had promised. The future held great wealth and great power if Gautama took the step to leave for the kingdom.

Gautama remained clear of mind and of quest. He would persist. He chose not to let the news of a possible, immediate threat to his clan and the loss of his ancestral kingdom disturb his emotions or his focus. He did not give in to the fear of loss, the fear of missing out on something that others sought so desperately, nor the greed of wanting it all.

Gautama entered a deep meditative state. He was seeking the truth about life itself. The true nature of life and happiness. Day after day passed. The gods gathered around to witness the enlightenment of the renunciant. Now Mara, the destroyer, sent his armies. They were charged with the single mission of disrupting the resolve and focus of the Buddha. They were determined not to allow Gautama to attain enlightenment. So they sent forth a terrible and terrifying storm to disturb the gathered gods and Gautama. The storm raged outside. Winds howled like demented demons. But the calmness inside did not waver. Gautama's inward journey continued uninterrupted. He was neither distracted nor disturbed.

Days passed as Gautama stuck fast to his determination and continued on his journey within. He deepened his concentration and focused his entire energy. His entire being was absorbed. It was now certain that enlightenment would be his, and he would know the meaning of life and happiness.

Mara, the tempter, then unleashed the dazzling beauty of his three daughters. One by one, they came. The first was Trsna, or Trishna, the desirable one. Stunning and tempting, she was the object of unending desire. Like her name, Trishna, which means desire or the thirst for more, she evoked the need to possess, to own and to consume. She danced and sang. Exposed her beautiful limbs, hoping to tempt the young man. The second was Rati, or the stunning beauty that promised complete fulfilment. After all, Gautama **was** seeking fulfilment, but of another kind, and here she held out the promise of fulfilment and completion that the entire world sought. The third was Raga, the embodiment of attachment. Her beauty was such that any man would fall in love with her, get attached to her and wish to possess her.

They sang the siren song of temptation and allure. They were dazzling and strong. Their beauty beyond description and beyond comparison. Perfect bodies, perfect faces and the promise of even more—sensual delights beyond imagination.

Gautama was indifferent to the allure that they held out. He chose to continue with his concentration and rejected the overtures. He was approaching the point of enlightenment.

Yet Mara would not give up. He tried again. This time it was Mara, as Dharma or Duty, who said to Gautama,

'Young man, the events of the world require your attention, and you will be remiss in your duty to your family and your clan if you do not take up the family responsibility. You will be remiss in your duty and your dharma (the code of honour, the code of conduct) if you do not immediately return to Kapilavastu, where your wife, child and ageing parents await you. They await you with anxiety and eagerness, holding fast to their hopes and dreams. Should you, in your moral quest, not consider this? Should you, in your moral quest, not shoulder these responsibilities? Should you, in your quest for enlightenment, give in to your selfishness by doing what you want and only seeking what you require?'

Gautama remained unmoved by this vivid picture and the criticism of his life choices. It was a criticism that would be levelled at him time and again. He had not quit his responsibilities. He was no quitter. He had made a different set of choices. He had moved beyond his responsibilities to his wife and newborn son to his higher responsibility—his inner awakening. And for the sake of this highest responsibility, he had persevered in the face of odds, in the face of doubt, in the face of troubles and in the face of the criticism that the world directed towards him.

As the forty-nineth day dawned, Gautama attained his goal and was now the Buddha, the enlightened one. Should he decide to share the way of enlightenment and happiness with others, it would spell failure for Mara and his forces. Much like the Dementors of Azkaban, Mara and his forces revelled in the misery, hopelessness and despair of people in the world. The Buddha's wisdom and his understanding of the true nature of the world would help people transform suffering into happiness, misery into wisdom and hopelessness into hope.

Mara, the master of delusion, appeared and congratulated Gautama the Buddha on succeeding in his search and on his enlightenment. Mara's voice was soft and mellow. His gaze was direct and even benign. Perhaps the Buddha would believe Mara was now aligned with his interests. Only then would Mara succeed in his work. Now, Mara shared his views with the Buddha. 'O enlightened one, it is a matter of delight and great joy that you have succeeded in understanding the truth of life. Of understanding the nature of the world. Of understanding the past, the present and the future. Now that you have attained this most marvellous understanding, you will also have understood that staying in this world is futile. After all, you have overcome all attachment, and all the fetters are shattered. I am sure you will directly enter Nirvana next.'

Nirvana, to cease the cycle of suffering in continual birth and death, was the goal. The Buddha did think of Nirvana and perhaps of leading a life immersed in his own awakening. He had to make a choice. To remain immersed within himself or engage in the difficult and even bitter struggle to share his understanding with others.

The common man or woman is not engaged in this quest at all and may even be indifferent to any teachings around it. Sharing his understanding and the path to inner awakening meant a great struggle would have to be embraced. He would have to devote the rest of his life on earth to doing just that. It was not the difficulty of it that was the deterrent, but . . . Was it worth it? Would anyone truly be interested? How would he do it? Where would he start?

Should he, the enlightened one, the Buddha, embark on this new struggle or let it be? The struggle promised to be a lifelong one, after all. There would be no going back. It was a commitment. It was a promise. Would it be worth it? Or should he enter Nirvana now?

GREAT EXPECTATIONS

HOLDING MINE LIGHTLY!

'Right vision consists in knowledge
concerning suffering, the cause of
suffering, the cessation of suffering
and the path that leads to the cessation of
suffering.'

—The Buddha (*Maha Satipatthana Sutta*)

The early evening dinner was a sumptuous spread, and we lingered over it. We had all gathered with a renewed sense of calm certainty that this retreat would give us clear answers to our questions and concerns.

I could see a few people approaching the portal's team and talking earnestly. 'Whatever is going on?' I wondered. I hoped all was well and there was nothing untoward to worry about. Riya was walking briskly to where Gautam stood, gazing at the inky darkness of the water. He was listening intently to Sumit and Meena.

I made my excuses and deftly pulled out of the small group with whom I had been chatting about my experiences and conversations with Gautam. I had been telling them about how he had been such a transformational and life-changing influence on me.

Just a few moments before I reached him, Gautam turned to look for me. Riya was a few steps closer to me. She said, 'Some of the group want to have an evening session with Gautam. I know it is not part of the plan to do a session now, but it seems to have the popular vote. In fact, they are insisting that we start as soon as dinner is done. What do you think?'

I could understand their impatience to find answers and solutions and to find them *now*. Gautam's voice, his bearing and the sharp clarity he brought to the understanding of relationships were remarkable. He offered the sanest and most profound perspectives. I told Riya I was game if the majority of the group wished to stay up and chat. And whoever wanted to opt out of the impromptu session was free to do so as well. We had travelled a distance, so naturally some of the folks could have been tired.

Riya and Sartaj left to make arrangements with the resort. We would have a closer group setting with candles on the long table and dessert and coffee service to conclude. The dinner would be moved to the pavilion for us. A few people still had demands for pizza. They carried their loaded plates out of the restaurant and onto the pavilion.

The clink of china and the rustle of clothing all faded away as Gautam entered, carrying a cup of tea with him. A frugal eater, he carried his daily discipline into the travel and time away and had long finished his dinner. He beckoned me to a seat closer to him and asked me to make sure that I continued chronicling the conversations. Yes, I surely would.

Gautam received undivided attention as he started to speak. 'This morning GP started or, as she says, kick-started, us off by noting down everyone's expectations. I thought perhaps we could chat about expectations. Expectations from our partners. And how we manage them. What do you think? Would that be of any interest to you?'

Yes, it certainly was of interest to us. Our keen nods and attentive body postures were dead giveaways. We were all looking forward to understanding this. Nearing the twelve-year mark myself in my marriage to Manu, I was all the more curious to know what Gautam would have to say. I knew I keenly felt the sharp and unforgiving edge of my own expectations from Manu. He was very much his own person and not someone to give in to cajoling or expectations to be or do certain things. I slowly and haltingly said as much. This was as much my contribution to getting the conversation going as it was a search for a solution to this rankling matter.

Stuti, a techie from Bangalore, was sipping her colourful cocktail as she said, 'You know, Gautam, expectations are definitely the big issue in any relationship. I have not succeeded with any strategy. I read somewhere that men like direct and clear statements. I have done that with ex-boyfriends and my ex-husband. I have also tried being subtle when that did not work. I have even tried giving up on my expectations, but I end up feeling frustrated when my partners don't respond. Nothing seems to work. I think it is hopeless to have any expectations at all from men. Or maybe it's me. Maybe I'm just a bit too strong and direct.'

Here was a good-looking, well-dressed and well-spoken woman in her prime. Surely she was doing well professionally and, therefore, financially. This retreat wasn't exactly cheap. And despite all she had going for her, romance and marriage had not been working out for her. Where are the guys, I wondered? And why are relationships so jinxed and difficult for some people? For so many others, they seem pretty seamless and easy, at least on the surface.

Stuti continued, 'Before anyone here thinks that I am having multiple relationships, this is all in the past. Nothing really worked out. At least not for the long term. My marriage ended after just eighteen months, even though we got married after some months of living together.

There were a few nods around. Dating was not easy. We all understood that and knew that from our own experiences.

Gautam said, 'And did you, Stuti, spend time with all the people you dated? Did you get to understand them well enough?'

Stuti nodded vigorously and said, 'Of course, Gautam. Of course. Very much so. I made it a point to really get to know these guys. I have never rushed into relationships. I did not rush into marriage as well. Perhaps I would have been better off if my parents had found a suitable boy for me and I had started out with zero expectations, which I believe is the case with arranged marriages.'

Vikrant, the good-looking banker from London, said, 'Let me assure you, Stuti, that arranged marriages carry their share of expectations too. There is no such animal as an expectation-free relationship. I have met so many girls through my parents and extended family, despite the fact that I have been living in Europe for the past seven years. Finally, I've decided to choose a partner that I am in love with. I have yet to sign up for a longer package with anyone, but I had heard so much about Gautam sir, that I was convinced that I must make the time and be here for these three days.'

Gautam flashed his amazing smile and said, 'Thank you, Stuti and Vikrant. I am so glad to have you both here. I hope that your expectations from the retreat are fulfilled here.

'Stuti, how exactly are your expectations not being met in your relationships? Anything you can briefly share with us will be wonderful.'

Stuti said, after a pause, 'I may need to think some more before answering this, Gautam, but I think most of the guys I was with were more into themselves than into me. They wanted me to follow their interests, which I did, but they did not step up to spend time with me the way I wanted. And the initial rush of romance just flies out of the window and goes into hiding forever after the first six to eight months. Even all that caring, sharing and telling me how wonderful I am. I guess the first flush of it all. Then I start feeling let down by their personalities, which begin to appear very one-dimensional to me.

'I have interests outside of work. I have a life outside of work. I love to cook, to dance, to attend theatre and sometimes I try my hand at stand-up comedy. The guys are interested only in work, sex and parties. They don't seem to want to do other things or explore anything new. I want someone who perfectly matches me in all my interests. Someone who has a high level of energy but also knows how to relax at home by diving deep into music or meditation.'

'Wow,' I thought to myself, 'Stuti is seeking a twin. It is an impossible ask. How and from where would she find someone who did it all, had it all and matched all these varied interests?' I turned to Gautam with great interest. The faces around me matched my curiosity. How would Gautam help Stuti? What magic wand would he wave so that Stuti would find her perfect match? Or wouldn't she?

Gautam was smiling at Stuti. In his characteristic way, he said, 'Let us say, Stuti, that you find someone who is just like you. With high energy. Good at so many things and has an equal interest in multifarious things. Good at work and matches your requirements for love and romance. Will that be a guarantee of happiness in any way? Being married to someone so multifaceted may, in fact, be somewhat tiring for you. Because you have all those qualities, someone else does not need to have them. You bring yourself and your A game to the equation. Just as your partner brings his.

'Among my close friends was Dr K.K. Aggarwal who passed away in 2021 due to COVID-19. Not only was he highly accomplished, acclaimed and awarded—he received the Padma Shri—but he also had a deep understanding of life and its issues. A modern sage, he was deeply wise. He once told me about the need in all of our lives for different kinds of friends. Friends whom we can look up to as mentors and guides, friends who share our interests and passions, the special someone with whom we can be ourselves and share intimacy and others who are fellow spiritual travellers. These were perhaps the five elements of intimacy in Draupadi's story in the Mahabharata.

'The problem arises when we start "dumping" or expecting it all from one person when we may actually need

The problem arises when we start 'dumping' or expecting it all from one person when we may actually need different types of friends and companions for our different interests.

different types of friends and companions for our different interests. And be prepared to invest in different levels of intimacy.

'I am not for a moment suggesting multiple sexual partnerships, but different folks and friends for different interests. So you can have a few friends or a group of friends who are as keenly interested in or knowledgeable as you about theatre because your partner does not share that interest. Or another set of friends who attend dance classes with you, or whatever else. It is actually okay to find and nurture friends for all these interests. The whole idea is to not dump all your expectations on one person. Of course, if you manage to find a multifaceted partner, that is wonderful, but if not, it does not bar you from enjoying marriage or a special someone in your life and celebrating your other interests either on your own or with other people.

'You have to be willing to shift your expectations, Stuti.'

Stuti's reluctance and frustration were evident in her facial expressions. They became even more evident as she said, 'But Gautam, that is the whole idea, isn't it? To have someone by my side and participating in my life. In all aspects of it. All the time'.

'No, Stuti. That cannot be the idea of an ideal marriage. Or the ideal relationship. Our life partners are not our twins or true copies. It is simply not possible. They are individuals with their own identities. Yes, you should have someone by your side. Participating in each and every aspect of your life? Not so much. Participating where they choose and in what is desirable or necessary, yes. And while I understand and even agree that having common interests is helpful, people change. Their interests and passions change over time. Then what will happen? Even you will change.

'The absence of common interests cannot be a deal breaker. I urge you, Stuti, to look within and understand where this is coming from. I think you are wiser than this. Do you make hiring decisions at work? For your team, I mean?'

'Yes,' Stuti replied.

'When hiring for your team, are you seeking people with complete homogeneity or some diversity? And which do you think is better for your team and for you as the team head?' Gautam asked softly.

The pin-drop silence was deafening. Even my breathing was slower than it had been.

As the silence grew longer, many others started muttering that diversity was better. Because it brought much more to the table. Including skills, insights and unique strengths. Stuti was doodling on the pad in front of her, and at last, she sighed, looked up at Gautam, and said in a forlorn voice, 'Diversity is better, of course. But does this mean I have been stupid about my choices? What do I do about the mistakes of my past?'

Gautam's voice carried a deep reassurance as he said, 'You have to start by seeing, actually seeing, the wonderful uniqueness and characteristics of your partner. Expecting them to be like you in each aspect is a notion that will bring you pain. Hold on to the expectations that serve you well. But I think it is time to question your expectations. How much does an unfulfilled expectation really matter? Can you go ahead and realize that need or that unfilled expectation on your own or with someone else? Is that possible?

> *Hold on to the expectations that serve you well.*

Not all expectations will be met. Not all unmet expectations are reasons to call off a relationship.

'Human nature being what it is, we think we will feel complete or whole because of others. But the truth is very different. We feel complete and whole because of ourselves. Our own efforts. It is okay—absolutely fine—to feel disappointed in someone else. Even to experience disappointment in life. What we choose to do after that is the key to our happiness, wholeness and feelings of contentment and fulfilment.

Human nature being what it is, we think we will feel complete or whole because of others. But the truth is very different. We feel complete and whole because of ourselves.

'You don't need a perfect relationship to be happy. You don't need the most perfect person to be fulfilled. You don't need someone else to complete you. You can be happy, fulfilled and content without this. People sometimes feel that their happiness is contingent upon this happening or that person responding in a certain way. And only then will they be happy.

'If we start accepting what others tell us and what culture conditions us to believe, happiness will be out of reach for most people because it depends on so much outside of us. Someone else—so many voices—are telling us how life ought to be. How our partners ought to be and how they ought to behave and fulfil us. There is so much that is out of our hands.

'I remember my friend GP here being so unhappy when her hubby, Manu, did not give her a special gift on their tenth wedding anniversary. Do you remember, GP, how much it disturbed you and created such a ruckus between the two of you? Would you like to share something from that with all of us?'

Well, Gautam had firmly raised the spotlight and rained it straight down on me. I almost squirmed with embarrassment and gave Gautam a look. But the warmth and encouragement on his face helped me calm down. Oh God! That had been a terrible time. My dad, then 90 years old, was ailing. He had been hospitalized and was recovering extremely slowly. I moved Dad to my place for his comfort and better quality of nursing and care. Not to mention more peace of mind for me. I knew I could do this like no one else.

Manu was travelling most of the time, leaving me alone to fend for myself during many difficult moments and critical medical-care decisions. I expanded my capabilities: I networked with all the doctors, got in touch with medical suppliers, identified an ICU-trained male nurse to be with my father 24/7 and set up a medical unit in my guest room.

Manu's insistence on travelling and the total dismissal of our tenth anniversary as a milestone were huge disappointments for me. Yes, it was clear that it was not the time for a celebration or throwing a party. No, that is not what I was expecting. I did expect his physical and emotional availability. I did expect far more hand-holding. I did expect an expensive gift on our anniversary. And my friends egged me on, saying that they were sure Manu would end up surprising me with at least a solitaire, if nothing else.

The more I insisted, the more distant Manu seemed and less inclined to give me anything expensive or even be around to support me emotionally.

Life left me aching and emotionally tossed up, given that my dad was so critically ill and my own disappointment at how things were with Manu.

I turned to Gautam for advice and was pretty much caught off guard by what he had to tell me. Gautam said, 'Forget the solitaire. You are unlikely to get it. Diamonds are not a reflection of love. Spouses who cheat on their partners can sometimes be far more generous. So just as their giving expensive and big gifts is not an indicator of their care and concern, neither is Manu's refusal to give you any gift whatsoever a sign of being uncaring. It is up to him to give or not. You are no beggar to keep asking for this, that and the other. **And** this insistence on him getting you stuff and gifting you jewellery will not work with force or repetition. If he feels like it, he will do it. Else forget it.'

I felt impatient with Gautam and said, 'No, Gautam. You are getting me wrong. It is not about asking or about greed. It is simply that these gestures will make me feel important. It will make me feel that I matter to him. That our tenth milestone means something to him. You don't think that our tenth wedding anniversary is special? If Dad had not been so critical and if he wasn't in the hospital earlier this past month, I would have even liked to host a party. But, of course, now is not the time.

'And I don't know if I have shared with you that earlier, Manu was big on gestures—he got me flowers all the time. Before our wedding, he was always excited to get me jewellery, and I still remember him going out of his way to buy me stuffed toys for Valentine's Day. Now all that has stopped. I think it is a matter of completely taking our relationship for granted. He doesn't call me as much when he is out or we are not together. He seems to have changed.'

Gautam said thoughtfully, 'Perhaps you are right. Maybe he has changed. Maybe he is taking you for granted. I understand how important a gift is at this special milestone as a sign and a symbol of how much you and this relationship mean to him. Congratulations, by the way. It's no small feat to reach the ten-year mark in togetherness.

'My point to you is that Manu is a certain way. You cannot change him. Yes, your expectations from him are not being met at this time. Yes, it is hurtful to you. Emotionally painful. But how are you going to move ahead from here? Is getting stuck and frozen on this point going to help **you** as a person? Is it going to help your relationship move forward? Let us say you choose to stay with Manu. Will you hold it against him for the rest of your lives together and even beyond? You certainly can. But how does it help?

'Persisting with this misery **and** even the memory of this misery will initially make you angry and hurt. Later, it will simply convert into helplessness and depression. You can choose to continue as it is, knowing it will rebound on you.

'Do you not remember when I introduced you to Padmashree Dr K.K. Aggarwal? And he had said to you then, in the context of stressful situations, "If we want to remain stress-free, we must either change the stressful situation or change our interpretation of it. There is no other way.'"

Yes, I did recall that very wonderful meeting with the illustrious doctor. I did recall, clearly, these lines from that meeting. I had, in fact, recorded the whole conversation for future use. No, I did not want to live in bitterness or misery or keep experiencing this disappointment in my marriage. But I was loath to drop the expectation of a meaningful gift from Manu.

Slowly, I said, 'Yes, Gautam. I understand that my unmet expectations will become even more painful. It will cause me a world of hurt. What exactly do you expect me to do? You want me to stop expecting anything at all from my husband? Is that what you advise? And how will that become possible? I don't think it is possible or realistic'.

Gautam said, 'No, GP. Not at all. Being human means expectations will always be a part of our lives and relationships. Don't stop expecting. Don't stop having expectations from Manu. Do stop hurting yourself over them.'

> *Being human means expectations will always be a part of our lives and relationships. Don't stop expecting. Don't stop having expectations from Manu. Do stop hurting yourself over them.*

And how would I ever get the ability or the wisdom to do what he asked?

Being happy does not mean that everything is perfect. It means that you've decided to look beyond the imperfections.

—Unknown

168

GAUTAM'S GUIDANCE

Gautam was always crystal clear in what he shared. In the matter of expectations as well, he had been his usual clear self with us.

He began by telling us to accept that it was not our partner's 'job' to live up to our expectations, except, of course, in the basic values and 'rules' of marriage. For instance, the expectation of fidelity was both a value and a rule of marriage. This extended to emotional, sexual and financial fidelity.

It was then important to use the other set of unmet expectations to work on myself and grow as a person. I had to list out the expectations that I had and sort them into two baskets. The vital and essential value-based ones, and the balance in the other basket.

Gautam encouraged me to chat, not confront or give ultimatums to Manu, about my first basket. And to find the right time and space to do it. The right time and space would be when my dad's medical issues were sorted out. When I was not tired or exhausted. When I would be sure that my tone and intent were free of bitterness or accusations. When I could trust myself to be calm enough to assure Manu that this was not an ultimatum in any way. When I could point out that some things were simply not about me or him but about **us**. The couple. The partners. The life partners that we had chosen to be.

Gautam asked me to strengthen my gratitude journal writing at that time and to make sure that one of the three points of the day was about Manu. So that I could clearly see what he was doing and what he was contributing. My previous emotional state made it easy to dismiss everything that he did on a daily basis. I had to be honest in making that one point about him. Whether it was his getting up earlier than me every single morning (when in town) to get the girls ready for school. Or the shouldering of our home loan EMI. Or the fact that not once did he withhold or begrudge the expense involved in looking after my dad.

It was important not to dump all my expectations on Manu. I had to be more outgoing and find different types of companions and friends for a host of activities that I was interested in. This was key—not dumping it all on one person.

I had to prioritize the expectations in the second basket. Rank them in order of importance, and then draw up a plan of action on how to achieve them. Since I wanted those things for myself, it was my job to provide them. So many things I always thought I needed from others were only within my control.

Gautam explained clearly that the more we rely on someone else to give us what we need, the more disempowered we feel. The further we are from happiness, the weaker our ability to fulfil ourselves on our own. And that it was okay to feel disappointed. Feeling disappointed from time to time is part of being human. Carrying that disappointment and holding on to it all the time was the big problem. It was vital to not become the cause of my own complaints in life and with Manu. No, I would choose to fulfil my expectations from the second basket. Yes, I would choose to remain happy in the course of my life and its shared elements.

FIGHT OR FLIGHT?

WHEN CONFLICT ARISES AS IT MUST

'If you wish to follow the Way, do not use force
to settle disputes. Instead calmly consider what
is right and wrong, looking at all sides of the
dispute. You should be concerned only with truth
and peace. The truth is your guardian and you
are the guardian of the truth. In this way you will
combine wisdom with virtue.'

—The Buddha (ascribed)

Day two of the retreat dawned bright. The sky and water were
a clear blue. The air smelled salty and oh so fresh. My lungs
were in danger of passing out—I was somewhat drunk on the
fresh air.

We were set to have an early breakfast on the beach.
The resort had set up a long table outside for us. And then
we could choose the time of the session before breaking for
a bit of a swim and scuba diving. It was a scramble to get
the early start after the travel and the late-night discussion.
But we were egged on by the fabulous spread of food and
fresh fruit.

The sun was dazzling even so early in the morning.
People were tugging on their shades. Beachwear casuals were
everywhere. Gautam wore a pristine kurta in the palest of
pink over worn denims. He looked marvellous. He could have
looked a bit out of place compared to everyone else, but such
was his aura and his way of carrying himself that he looked
natural, easy and charming.

I was keen to go back to my original thought of discussing
the elements of love. We'd already had a discussion on

commitment. Perhaps we could now discuss the elements of intimacy and passion. But the topic seemed a bit vague. I checked in with Riya, and she was nodding away, agreeing with me. Yes, we should look at pegging it around there. But she knew the group now had its own energy and might choose something entirely different.

Knowing Gautam somewhat well, I knew enough by now to know that he would also be open to suggestions from those present. Transformative conversations, he would say, are alive and sentient beings. They have a life of their own. A purpose of their own. Because they are capable of transforming those present. Because they speak of the truth inherent in life.

We trooped into the pavilion. The long, sheer curtains were tied back, and the French windows were opened to let in the muted voice of the mighty water and the freshest of breezes. Perhaps the resort thought that breakfast ought to be ongoing because some of the dry cakes, crackers and cheese, some small nibbles and a little fruit were laid out next to the large bottles of water and the tea and coffee service. Other than the fruit, everything was finger food or could be kept in the saucer of the tea and coffee cups.

Kareena, one of the programme participants, was a bright and pretty woman. Petite in build, she was well dressed and carried herself with terrific assurance in towering high heels. I would have lost my balance had I tried them. She spoke even before anyone else could say Good Morning and settle down: 'I belong to a small town, and my family is well to do. After studying overseas, I came back thinking marriage would be easy enough, as that is what my family wanted for me. I got formally engaged to a family friend's son, who lives in Manhattan. But we very quickly started experiencing so much conflict. We were arguing more than talking. Fighting more than flirting. The courtship itself appeared to be going nowhere and was filled with acrimony.

'It became so bad that everything said or unsaid was sparking a quarrel between us. We were fighting all the time, and finally I just could not handle it anymore. We parted ways. It has been three years since then, and despite having everything in my favour, I have simply not been able to get married. When I approached the portal, they said to try out this retreat to understand myself a little better. And before Riya jumps in, they did not promise that the retreat itself would help me get married but that it would be helpful in life.

'So here I am with all of you. And I am very glad that I made this choice. I feel more positive about myself and my own ability to be happy in life. I know that GP has given us the agenda to discuss intimacy and passion, but I just want to know more about how to handle relationships and how to handle conflict and fights. I don't want conflicts to stalk my footsteps. I don't want fights. Marriage or relationships become toxic when there is no peace and constant fighting. If the rest of you don't mind, I request that we discuss this issue. Please . . .'

We were all nodding in agreement. There was no great opposition from anyone, though a couple of guys cheekily said that they really wanted to get to the topic of passion and intimacy as soon as possible. Of course they would! Men will be men, I thought with amusement. A couple of others seconded the intimacy and passion bit as well, but the majority were keen on understanding how to handle conflict.

So, how was one to view conflicts in intimate relationships?

Gautam turned to me and said, 'GP, you have been researching and studying conflict between partners in marriage. What do you have to share with us? What is causing all this conflict?'

Once again, I found myself in the spotlight, and the question caught me off guard. Of course, I had done my homework. And research was something I was really good at, even outstanding at. However, sometimes being caught off guard makes me fumble a bit. I started speaking and hoped that my thoughts would fall into place soon.

'Well, Gautam. There are three sets of issues or concerns that set off arguments and fights. The first set is about the daily stuff—who is doing what chores to help around the house or not, who is littering around the house, and whatever else. This runs the gamut from who is pulling the covers to one side of the bed, hogging all the space, turning up the air conditioning when the other needs it down or up, or whatever else. It is about the daily grind and the daily friction in the machinery of living together. It becomes specific to living together and then perhaps raising children together or having pets together.

'The second set of issues is about a lack of intimacy. Yeah, yeah, I know I have been going on about it, but its absence is keenly felt, and it is an expectation that somehow women seem to feel the absence of more.

'Apart from intimacy or a lack thereof, this set of issues contains the potential for huge problems—conflicts over parenting, over money, over infidelity and even just growing apart and wanting to pull away. Substance abuse, alcoholism, bad company, gambling, credit card debt and compulsive disorders of all kinds, including shopping, eating and what have you. A complete absence of affection and interest. No sex, or even the wrong kind of sex. No communication or poor communication. Long spells of unemployment and, therefore, a fallout on finances, physical and mental health, and a host of other problems that accompany long-term unemployment.

'The third set of problems is more interesting and very modern. I have based it on my experience and observations. Traditional lists of problems between couples don't really spell it out. I think the biggest threat to togetherness comes from how we spend time on our devices and sometimes on our passions to the exclusion of all else. Is it gaming? Or even golf?

Or just streaming and binge watching? If it creates a divide between the couple, there is a problem brewing. Friction and conflict are the results.'

Riya was the first to speak: 'So glad to have you along, GP. That is pretty thorough and comprehensive. You have really done your homework.'

Stuti and Meena were clapping as I paused to take a few deep breaths. Gautam's smile made the effort of the deep dive worth it.

I had done my research as thoroughly as possible. I had also spoken with a few psychologists to understand conflict. And yet I worried about leaving something out. No list, however comprehensive, could ever claim to be the most definitive or complete one. It was possible that I may have missed out on a point or two. I said as much.

'Besides,' I added, 'I have not touched upon the cases of abuse. Physical and emotional abuse. Even verbal abuse is violence, after all. I feel that those cases need to be addressed differently. I hope that is fair to our discussion.'

Gautam chimed in decisively, 'Fair enough, GP. I agree that violence, abuse and living with someone who has a problem with substance abuse all fall into a different set of problems. Violence and abuse must not be put up with at all. Get out of an abusive relationship as soon as that abuse starts or you notice the signs of a violent temperament.

'Now, what do all of you think about the first basket of problems and the potential for fights and arguments there? What do you think is the solution? The best way to resolve these arguments and conflicts?'

There was a scramble to speak and share views on this.

Stuti was the first to go: 'I think the best way to handle this is to just keep reminding the other person of what they need to do. And hope that one day it will make a difference. I mean, what can you do if the other person is pulling the covers to one side or not putting the toilet seat down?'

Meena was smiling and relaxed as she answered, 'No, Stuti. With 19 years of experience, let me tell you that is not an approach that works well or at all. The more you remind a man of what you need him to do, the more irritated he gets, and from the smaller issue, it just spirals into something else.'

Yup, I thought. Meena had this dead to rights. Manu was careless with a few things and inattentive. He would forget things that were important to me. Whenever I reminded him about something, he would invariably snarl back, not wanting me to pressurize or nag him. That was never my intent. His snarl would ignite my irritation, and soon we would be in a slanging match.

Why, oh why had Gautam never spoken of managing fights and conflicts **before** I got married? Singlehood had its own set of difficulties, and being partnered had its own! Neither was an easy or comfortable state of affairs. Sigh!

What was to be done? I was looking to Gautam to provide the solutions, just like everyone else.

He smiled and said, 'Let us call the first basket defined by GP as daily stuff. These are not conflicts or fights. They are the smaller, daily expectations you have from your partner.

'One of the things to do is define these expectations at a time when tempers are not high. When the partner is not watching TV or on a work call, nor when you are in a hurry, hungry, tired or otherwise impatient or overwhelmed with something else. Take time out to discuss house rules when things are on an even keel. Let us say it is about specifying a routine that you want. So, specify. And do keep in mind that we all like minimal effort and minimal change. So don't be overwhelming. A change or two at a time. Specific changes, limited to one or two things, that require minimal effort.

'What is more important is that this is not about blame. "You have not been paying attention." "Why do I have to keep saying it . . . doing it . . ." "You will never change." are not the right things to either say out loud or even voice to yourself. People around us and our partners all respond to vibes. Our relationships mirror us. So don't carry the feeling that the other person is dumb, stupid or never going to change. Their not doing this daily stuff is not an indication of their love and affection for you. It is more about their journey in life. So don't make it out to be bigger than it is. Yes, it is irritating. Yes, I get it.

'Switch to positive attention. Attention to what they do. Attention to them. And an appreciation for any change, however small it may seem. And then have the patience to wait it out. Change does not happen in a day. Let us at least give it six months, or even a year.

'One of the most powerful things to do is to ask for help. Yes, they were supposed to have done it in the first place. You are carrying an equal load. You want your partner to as well. You discussed the whole thing in a reasonable way, at the right time, and even used a reasonable tone. But it did not happen. So how about doing it together? Not as a punishment to your partner but so that a certain rhythm sets in. And the right focus is given to what is left undone in the first place.'

There were smiling nods from all around. Yes, this was making sense. Of course, punishments simply did not work on some people. I remembered the time I stopped speaking with Manu over something, and it carried on for about three days. He continued to behave and speak as normally as ever. Whether I responded or not. Exasperated, I finally told him off and said, 'I am not speaking to you. I have not spoken to you since Wednesday, and today is Saturday. So just drop it.'

At which Manu said, 'Oh, I did not realize that you were not speaking to me. I thought everything was normal.' As I said earlier, Manu had Gautam to thank for an increased life expectancy! I could have cheerfully strangled him just for this one careless dismissal of my anger, hurt and withdrawal. One he hadn't even noticed.

'Conflicts are bound to happen. There will be quarrels, arguments and differences. If a couple can resolve these differences between them without involving someone else, any third person, that is the best. Only the couple knows what is really hurting between the two of them. Sometimes it is a mistake when the couple involves their friends, family and other people. Everyone else gives advice from their point of view and perspectives are very different. I believe in talking things out but not when both people are angry, when you are angry. That anger will not allow you to think straight or logically or from your own point of view. Talk once the anger has died down. As long as you can solve the differences between the two of you, it is the best.'

—Shibani Kashyap (in a personal chat)

Riya took me by surprise when she spoke up. The duo from the portal had been quiet all this time. Their interactions were limited to logistics and managing the work behind the scenes. They were not participating in the discussion as such.

'Even though I understand what you are saying, Gautam, I always end up fighting with my husband. He does not clean the bathroom after his bath, and his shaving stuff always messes up the sink and the counter. He drops his wet towel on the bed. And always, always on my side of the bed! It just drives me crazy. He needs to travel a lot and always does his packing on my side of the bed, claiming it is closer to the closet and the bathroom. I am very particular about cleanliness, and I have read so much about never placing used suitcases on the bed, but he always does it. What should I do?'

'Couples with a ratio of fewer than 5 positive interactions for every negative one are destined for divorce.'

—Relationship scientist John Gottman
(not in a personal chat)

Gautam responded: 'First of all, Riya, understand where you are coming from. Where are the irritation and anger coming from? Do they stem from the feeling that he is dismissive of what is important to you? Is it because you feel that, despite you having told him this countless times, he is simply careless? Careless of your feelings, perhaps?

'Sometimes our resistance creates a strange persistence in the behaviour of the other. If you give up your resistance for some time—one month or two—observe if it helps bring about a change. Take time out and talk to him about how it makes you feel. Share those articles about not placing suitcases on the bed. And what it does to the bed.

'Dissociate his behaviour from your own interpretation of what it means. It does not have a profound meaning or run any deeper than carelessness or force of habit. It has no bearing on the relationship at all. Certainly, the irritation and subsequent shouting will impact the relationship. Be extra attentive and loving whenever these things are done right by your partner. This is **not** being manipulative in any way, but simply helping them understand that you have paid attention and noticed when they made an effort.'

According to relationship scientist John Gottman, 69 per cent of a typical couple's fights are perpetual, based on core differences and cannot be resolved.

Even before Gautam could pause to take a breath and continue, people began prompting him about the second and third baskets of problems. Clearly, those were the deal breakers and of interest to everyone.

It was a more thoughtful Meena who started off by asking Gautam, 'Gautam, clearly my life falls into the second basket. Sumit cheated on me. Each moment, I'm grappling with thoughts about leaving him and filing for divorce. Should I do so? What is your advice on divorce?'

Gautam's answer was slow to come but clear as always: 'Divorce is a choice. A decision born of free will. And entirely up to the two people in the marriage. Just as entering into a relationship with someone is a matter of free will. A choice you make and exercise. There is no right or wrong here. It is what you choose to do. Your choice has to work well for you. That's all.

> *Divorce is a choice. A decision born of free will. And entirely up to the two people in the marriage. Just as entering into a relationship with someone is a matter of free will. A choice you make and exercise. There is no right or wrong here. It is what you choose to do. Your choice has to work well for you. That's all.*

'Would disappointment be my point of departure (from marriage or a relationship)? You have to find your own threshold. Each one must determine what is right for them. What they are ready to put up with.'

—Raga D'Silva (in a personal chat)

'Meena, the question you will need to answer for yourself is whether divorce will bring you peace. Your quest must be to heal from this wound. To find peace and calmness. Neither your anger at Sumit, however justified, nor your bitterness towards your cousin will magically go away with a legal or physical separation.

'The Buddha said that there are many kinds of suffering, of *dukkha*. There is "the suffering of having to meet with those whom one hates". This is acute suffering. A torment. And it may just make you feel helpless and enraged. The question is not whether to divorce or live with Sumit. The question is how to overcome this suffering and how to heal.

'And you can only do that by starting a new journey of forgiveness. And if you need help doing that, GP here has had her own journey of forgiveness and healing from great trauma. You can always check in with her on how to heal and move ahead in life. It will require effort and time on your part. But it will set you free of this suffering.

'I say to all of you, don't settle for a toxic relationship, but don't be in a rush to label a relationship as toxic. Labels take away our peace and happiness. Everyday friction is a part of life. It is your filter that will colour it a certain way. But it may not be hopeless.

'We cannot expect relationships to unfold exactly as we would like them to.

Blame is like putting your car in reverse and moving away from the direction you would like your life and partnership to go. Blaming your partner and constantly complaining about them makes you a victim. Endless blame makes you an endless victim.

'Those are assumptions and even expectations. Blame is like putting your car in reverse and moving away from the direction you would like your life and partnership to go. Blaming your partner and constantly complaining about them makes you a victim. Endless blame makes you an endless victim. As much as possible, try to resolve issues between the two of you. The moment a third person enters the picture, it changes the dynamic of the duo. You live your own reality, such as it is. And again, I say to you that I am not including abusive, violent or extreme cases here.

> *The problem is that we often fall into labelling things and behaviours as 'right' or 'wrong'. These labels create a bigger problem because you have made it a right-versus-wrong matter.*

'The problem is that we often fall into labelling things and behaviours as "right" or "wrong". These labels create a bigger problem because you have made it a right-versus-wrong matter. And guess where your partner is? Usually in the wrong. The other person will always be different from you. The other is different. Even your mirror image is different from you. Human nature quickly judges others as wrong, and that label creates dissonance and negativity.

'They are not wrong because they are not a certain way with you. They are just not as you would like them to be. They are being themselves. But your mind is labelling it "wrong" or "right".

'The most powerful way to remove the label is to enter into a dialogue with the other person, your partner. Ask yourself if every fight ends with ultimatums. The ultimatum is not about shouting out loud about a divorce. It is also about feeling like the other person is hopeless or that you are going to explode sooner rather than later because of the stress or unhappiness they have caused you.

'Dialogue is about learning to see life and life's issues from the perspective of the other. It is not about an ultimatum of divorce but about creating a safe space where a difference of opinion does not threaten the relationship in its totality.

'Addictions and destructive patterns of behaviour are not for you to change. You simply cannot. If someone is addicted to running their life on credit-card debt or gambling and you are footing the bill without their economic contribution or support, you need to ask yourself whether the relationship is still valid and whether you want to continue with it. Your fights, pleas or general appeals to their better nature are unlikely to make any change.

'Change happens when people walk themselves into change. Anyone trying to force a change on the other is doomed. Relationships of control and forced change are hellish for both people.

'If an argument does erupt, focus only on that topic. In other words, argue only about one thing at a time. Seek time out for a dialogue with the right intent and an openness to the other. They are also likely stressed or struggling in other areas of their lives outside of your relationship. Trying to change the other person creates hell in relationships. Remember that the only person whose behaviour and attitude you **can** change is yours. And only you can change yourself. Because you want to or need to.

> 'People are generally better persuaded by the reasons which they have themselves discovered than by those which have come into the mind of others.'
>
> —Blaise Pascal

'We tend to get personal or nasty in our frustration. And sometimes our defensiveness makes us want to lash out. It **does** make us lash out. This is hurtful. It is hurting the relationship itself. And weakening it in very subtle ways.'

The silence spoke volumes. I let it continue. What was the rush or the need to end it? It was a visibly calmer Meena who asked, 'Gautam, I know you have said that divorce is a matter of an individual's choice. But really, on what does one base the decision? How does anyone arrive at it? And no, I am not talking about the extreme or obvious cases. I just want to understand this better.'

Gautam had walked across the pavilion to pick up a bottle of water and was deeply drinking from his bottle. Wanting to give him a much-needed break, I hastily interjected, 'Just sharing something from research once again—half of divorces happen in the first ten years of marriage. The rate of divorce is especially high between the fourth and eighth anniversaries. And, interestingly enough, more women file for divorce than men. This is quite a global trend, not just in any one country. Something like 70 per cent of divorce cases are filed by women. Life tends to be easier for men post marriage. They have access to regular sex, better food and better care. There is someone to either do or share domestic responsibilities and chores with. Besides, women tend to be more nurturing. This increases men's satisfaction with marriage and makes marriage more agreeable.

'But lopsided responsibility may make marriage more stressful for women and more demanding physically and emotionally. As more women have stressful working conditions and more professional demands on them, their lives become more complicated. This makes marriage tougher to cope with. It is only a man's support and care that can make marriage a better and more workable proposition for the woman.'

I paused to take a breath. Gautam was smiling with kindness. As if he knew I had rushed in to support him. I smiled back and subsided. It was over to him now. Gautam said, 'If divorce is happening without it being an extreme case, it should happen because no one could have done anything more to save the relationship. The question you need to ask yourself and answer with complete honesty is, 'Have I truly done all that I could to save this relationship? Have I truly done all that I could to serve this relationship? Have I been fair to both of us? To us? Why am I willing to give up on us? Has she or he stopped adding any value at all to my life, or have I stopped adding value to myself?

'For instance, if the husband stops his wife from having a field job or an assignment that takes her away from home for weeks on end, it can be contentious. But what if that forced change compels the wife to start learning something new or take a course in digital marketing, apply for jobs and get one?

'And it turns out to be the better-paying and more fulfilling option. Now that the very same element has transformed from controlling and toxic behaviour to something that pushes her to become better and more independent, there is actually reason to be grateful to the husband. Not divorce him. Because he compelled her to become independent. To acquire more and different skills. Of course, if the control and toxicity continue, then separation is an option for the wife.

'Divorce if you must. Even divorce can be a lesson for life. People learn things they could not have or even would not have learned in any other way. This learning helps them go on to make far stronger relationships and marriages than they might otherwise have made.

> *Divorce if you must. Even divorce can be a lesson for life. People learn things they could not have or even would not have learned in any other way. This learning helps them go on to make far stronger relationships and marriages than they might otherwise have made.*

'You don't have to be tied together for the rest of your lives, holding on to and building resentment.

'I always say one must marry only for the right reasons. Today I add to that. Divorce only for the right reasons. Neither marriage by itself nor divorce are good or bad. They simply are. How we "use" marriage to create happiness for ourselves and others and how we "use" divorce to create value in life are key. Neither should make us lesser people. Only better people.'

'For me, red flags are alcoholism, violence, aggression. When dealing with heartbreak or rejection, it is about learning from it.'

—Raga D'Silva (in a personal chat)

THE ARMIES OF MARA

THE ARSENAL OF TEMPTATION

The workings of the universe are subtle. It is a battlefield with an unceasing tug of war between the good and the bad. Between the forces that seek to bring us down and those that allow us to fly free. Between happiness and unhappiness. Between suffering and calmness. Between expectation and acceptance.

In a universe filled with battlefield upon battlefield, the biggest battlefield of all is the human mind. Conflicting thoughts and vicious emotions that inflict violence on the body. It all unfolds and happens in the human mind. Losing the battle of the mind is painful. And all leads to loss: loss of opportunity, loss of relationships, regrets over could-have-beens and should-have-beens . . . Mara, the destroyer, uses his armies skillfully in the human mind. Losing therefore becomes a matter of giving up and giving in to what the Buddha termed 'unskillful emotions'. In Sanskrit, the term is *kalesh*, while in Pali, it is referred to as *kalesa*.

What are actually unskilful emotions? What do they do?

The Buddha described all that is unhelpful to progress and happiness, or obstacles and hindrances, as unskilful. Our quest is for happiness—happiness in life and happiness in love. It all depends on how we feel and how we perceive our lives to be progressing.

Progress depends on our choices of action, words and even thoughts. With progress, a feeling of contentment and happiness emerges from within. Happiness, then, is a skill and the result of progress, perspective and choice. The Buddha taught this nearly 2600 years ago, and today, modern science concurs. Unskilful emotions are those that take us away from progress and, therefore, happiness. Unskilful emotions keep us from choosing happiness or sustaining happiness over the long term.

Unskilful emotions take us to a negative plane of action and reaction. To make the wrong choices. Choices that are inimical to happiness. Choices that lead to anger and despair. Despair leads to losing heart, losing the right opportunity, and losing the opportunity to grow and evolve. Winning over instinct, despair and 'unskilful' emotions by developing a larger heart and a constructive approach is victory. It leads to happiness, fulfilment of desire, better relationships and a better life.

Winning over instinct, despair and 'unskillful' emotions by developing a larger heart and a constructive approach is victory. It leads to happiness, fulfilment of desire, better relationships and a better life.

Ours is a universe where the laws of gravity (with its downward pull) and aerodynamics (with its lift and its ability to defy gravity) coexist. Each has a role and its own unique mission. This polarity is reflected in the play of light and shadow, in positivity and negativity, in the constructive and the destructive. Both polarities have roles to fulfil.

It is Mara and his armies—those unskilful emotions and even unhelpful attitudes, the *kalesa*—that enable the negative and the destructive to fulfil their mission. Just like the seismic forces that cause earthquakes and tsunamis that are below the entire surface of the Earth, these negative and destructive forces underlie each moment, each element of the mind, and our response. The underlying seismic forces wait and watch for weakness along the earth's crust before erupting in their destructive frenzy (as quakes and tsunamis). The negative and destructive forces in our lives wait and watch for the weakness in our approach, in our conduct, and in our character to erupt and unleash a frenzy of destruction. And both can destroy in a matter of moments, sweeping away the work and effort of a lifetime.

Mara, as you know by now, is the name of the god of destruction and death. His role in the universe is to rule minds and human beings through the armies he brings. He uses myriad forms and means to lure human beings away from happiness. He skilfully uses human nature to do that. Doubt arises from within—this is too good to be true, it says. You are too tired or too old to try this new way of living. You are simply not lucky in love. And so on . . . Mara's army uses our personalities and our tendencies to make us lose our way in life and move away from the path of progress.

The first of the forces of Mara is that of **sensual pleasure**. It urges human beings to give in to temptation and experience pleasure—unending, relentless, alluring, tempting and, of course, justifiable in its own way—to win. Be it lust, be it greed for more or even the desire for something different, or the use of an opportunity that simply presents itself and is too good to be true, it is desire at work. Desire creates effort but also brings attachment to the false and the ever-changing.

Interestingly enough, the second of the forces is **discontent and boredom**. This is at the root of a whole lot of mischief in the world. In the matter of relationships, it can be the driving force behind wrong choices with a partner, in casual sex and in extramarital relationships. Boredom often spells a marriage's doom. Discontent and boredom are both dangerous, and keeping them at bay calls for conscious and deliberate effort in the way we lead our lives. This conscious and deliberate effort is called mindfulness.

The third of Mara's forces is **hunger and thirst**. Hunger and thirst in today's times, and perhaps for the readers of this book, may be lower priorities. But in the time of the Buddha, those engaged in the quest for enlightenment found themselves distracted and interrupted by hunger and thirst. Today, our electronic devices and social media fall into this category of being major distractions and interruptions in our quest to build happiness in our lives.

Craving is the fourth weapon in the arsenal of Mara and his armies. It marches closely with discontent and with sensual pleasures. Combined, they all urge us on for more and more. Even better and better. This craving is never satisfied. It compels us to not just reach for the extra-large helping or slice of chocolate cake but also to make the wrong choices in finding the right date or continuing with a toxic relationship. And, of course, continuing with that extramarital relationship is only going to hurt and damage lives.

A potent force in our life is our will or our determination. But it is overcome by this fifth soldier: **laziness or inertia**. The Buddha's description is closer to the English equivalents of sloth and torpor. We may know that our bodies need exercise. We understand that we will benefit from the sustained effort to be online in finding the right partner. We know with certainty that we have much work to do on ourselves, for instance, in paying our credit-card bill on time, so we can be easy on the financial front. But we just don't make the time for what we say is important to us, for what will help us become fitter, healthier and even richer.

This sixth army of Mara is a real killer. It is **fear.** It can leave us paralysed just when action is called for. It stops us from exploring and living life to the fullest. It stops us cold in our tracks.

The seventh troop is that of **doubt or indecisive wavering.** The human mind is fickle and given to doubt quite naturally. Social narratives add to this by dampening our instincts, our gut feelings and our higher selves, all of which could actually lead us to a different and better life, better decision-making and better results.

This next army of Mara is one of **restlessness.** There are several examples of the damage caused by it, and many texts refer to it as conceit and ingratitude. Whatever its name—

restlessness, conceit or ingratitude—it creates cracks in our relationships. It is a powerful driving force in human life. Conceit can bring about rigidity in our interactions with others, while ingratitude kills happiness and relationships. Unfortunately, both conceit and ingratitude abound in the modern world. And within us.

Falsely received gain, renown and **honour** are the ninth army brought to bear on the human condition by Mara. Consciously choosing to receive false gain and honour does not lead to happiness. It moves us further away from contentment and our own evolution.

The last and final missile in Mara's arsenal is **arrogance and putting others down or disparaging others** while extolling one's own self. It is immediately clear that this can be damaging to our close relationships.

Each of these is distinct and has a clear role to play in our lives and minds. Self-awareness is the first step to defeating the armies of Mara.

WANTING WHAT YOU HAVE

THE EBB AND FLOW OF DESIRE

> 'Love at first sight is easy to
> understand; it's when two people
> have been looking at each other for a
> lifetime that it becomes a miracle.'
>
> —Amy Bloom

Time flowed by through the gradients, slopes and valleys of life. Sometimes crystal clear and many times muddy, often turbid with disturbances of life and emotions.

Manu and I had moved through life and its myriad forms. The loss of our parents. The loss of my income and the struggle to earn more. The cares of being caregivers to our surviving parents. To our siblings. To our daughters. To each other. And, finally, to ourselves.

Responsibility upon responsibility. Many of which we had chosen to accept and shoulder ourselves. There was no precedent that forced us. That compelled us to take this on ourselves. No precedent whispered its insidious tune of how things **ought** to be. And what people would say.

No external voice or external force would have compelled me to look after my father. It was my choice to do so. Just as it was Manu's to visit his mom every day and eat lunch with her, driving a considerable distance back and forth. Initially, he did this to soothe his mom's sensitivities about moving out of the home post-marriage. And when she was diagnosed with cancer, he chose to continue looking after her, getting her the right treatment and cheering her up. He did this even though two of his sisters were living with his mother.

We were now expert jugglers. Juggling our marriage and our relationship with looking after family. Juggling our work and professions with all the other stuff that was going on. There was simply a whole lot that had happened and was happening. Life did not always allow for romance and handholding. Even sex would fall by the wayside as we battled our way through all that life flung at us.

Intimacy and sex went further and further from my mind as my corporate career came to a hard stop. The shift to unemployment was a huge downturn for me. And from a very comfortable double-income couple, the onus was suddenly all on Manu. A new struggle, a new era of our relationship, was starting. And it took Manu further away. Physically. Geographically. Mentally. Emotionally.

He was putting in long hours at his new factory and office. He was travelling. He was now sharply focused on his business and on growing it. I felt lonelier than ever. His physical absence left me struggling—to cope with raising our two young daughters, managing the home singlehandedly, and caring for my dad and my brother as well. His emotional absence left me struggling with my feelings and the events of my life. I felt lonely and even abandoned.

I could feel once more the deep, dark pull of feelings of hopelessness. Manu's presence at home and in town did not bring any happiness or alter my situation in any way. It did not cheer me up or lighten my emotional burden.

Was this the end of my dreams and desires? Would we always be steeped in life and our cares? Would we someday reconnect with each other? Was there a way or a method to reignite the passion between us and fan the embers of romance? Was this the end of the road for us as a couple? Perhaps it was time to accept life as it was unfolding. And why did I expect that there would still be romance lurking in a decade-plus marriage?

When I looked around, I could see a similar tiredness in other couples. I could see that women found solace and camaraderie in their friendships, not so much in their marriages. Many, it seemed, had plunged wholly into their roles as mothers and homemakers. Several others spent long hours in the beauty salon and working out, achieving great results. Was it a way of life, a choice or a way of filling the void within? Men were immersed in their careers, travels and buddies. Some in their hobbies, devices and investments. And some were focused on their children's academics or careers. But not many men were concentrating on their relationships and partners.

I knew I was not alone in my misery or the issues in my marriage. I had always prided myself on my ability to seek answers and find solutions. After all, I had been able to rise like the phoenix both personally and professionally. But life's blows—heck, the process of life itself—had taken a toll. I felt tired and weary. Too dispirited to seek answers. Too stressed and careworn to find solutions. What was the way forward for me? Getting the right employment opportunity was not in my hands. Living in limbo is simply not an option. The work for the retreat and putting together the white paper around it had been energizing, but soon it would be just a distant memory. I was close to wrapping it all up and handing it in.

I was concerned about my relationship with Manu. He and I had always enjoyed the intimacy of our relationship. The talks, the handholding and, of course, sex. I knew that too long a gap without intimacy would eventually take a toll on the health of our relationship. I thought of starting a little project to research desire. How could one keep it alive and well in a relationship? How could I bring back desire? What really impacted desire?

That afternoon, I was desultorily trying to start on research and a bit of writing. I had found the phone to be a huge distraction. Picking up the phone meant a loss of time. It would leave me hard-pressed to get back to my own intent for the day and how I had planned to spend my time.

Déjà vu! It was sheer chance that I spotted Gautam's message. He was inviting me to lunch.

His message was like the sun breaking through the gloom of my life. Within moments, I felt like a new person. Was it the prospect of stepping out of the house? Doing something new? Perhaps a bit of both. Just being purposeful was good.

How marvellous the human mind is, I thought to myself. I had gone from a state of moodiness to one of well-being in a snap. I rushed to get ready. My step-out-of-the-house clothes. The right bag and shoes. Studs on my ears. A spritz of rose water, and I was ready. How marvellous and how fickle! How quick to experience this change of feelings and emotions. In the snap of a moment. Truly, it was as the Buddha had taught millennia ago.

As I walked into the café, I was struck by the small group around Gautam. Sumit and Meena were there. I was somehow not surprised to find them. I knew that they would have reached out to Gautam to help them put life into perspective. Especially Meena, given how deeply affected she had been. And how deeply disturbed! Riya from the portal was there, as were Vikrant and Kareena. I nearly thought I would end up seeing the whole shebang. What? Were we starting another retreat? Why had no one told me?

Moving closer to the table, I could see Vikrant and Kareena were sitting close. Something about the aura around them . . . romance was in the air! Perhaps it was only to be expected. They were so confident and vibrant. They looked good together. The whole purpose and point of the retreat had been to understand love and relationships, whether to better them or start them. To find love. Silently, I wished them well and hoped it would turn out to be a wonderful and long-lasting relationship.

It turned out that Vikrant and Sumit were hosting the lovely impromptu lunch as a thank you to Gautam, Riya and me. It explained the smaller numbers. A cosier setting than the larger group at the retreat. And what a wonderful thought! I wished I had known a bit in advance. I would have liked to carry small presents or mementos for everyone.

The first flush of romance, togetherness and, er, intimacy was all too evident between Kareena and Vikrant. The looks and smiles. The casual touch every now and then. Aww . . . I was reminded of how it had been between Manu and me years ago. Aeons ago. I wondered if it would ever be the same. Surely there was a way to recapture the magic and wave the wand over both of us, over our 'settled' togetherness?

Yes, I was doing all that I had learned from Gautam. Yes, there were occasions and opportunities for romance, intimacy and sex. But not only did they not present themselves all the time; life's ups and downs and our own mood of the moment did not allow us to make the most of them. If only there was a way to be more consistent.

The urgency of my own feelings was such that I interrupted the ongoing chat with the seemingly random, 'It is so wonderful, so marvellous to see Kareena and Vikrant. You guys are so in love. It is almost enviable. It makes me want to revisit my past and fall in love all over again.'

I thought the interjection was rather weird. But no one else seemed to. Riya said, 'Isn't it just marvellous? I wish you guys all the luck. And like GP here, I caught myself envying you two in this phase of your relationship. It is simply the best. Make the most of it and create as many deep memories of it as possible. I have been married for six years now, and I've noticed how things have changed over the years. I wish I could travel back in time and recreate those months and years of courtship, romance and sparkling love.

'No, don't get me wrong. I still love Chetan, my hubby. We have been together since college. Our friendship is still strong, but . . . Gautam, is there something I can do, or something we can all do to recapture that sparkling feeling? What do you think? I really thought we might be able to talk at length about this at the retreat, but it never came up. Everyone had different needs. Everyone wanted to talk about different things.'

Gautam was smiling, as composed and calm as ever. I had fully expected to find him in his usual white tee and denims, but it was a long linen kurta with a spotless white churidar that was his look for the day.

'I understand what you are saying, Riya. Yes, it is a concern. Starting married life on such a lovely note and then finding it getting diluted with time. Living a loving life is worth exploring at length. I am willing to chat with as many people as are interested. Do you think it is a good thing to put it out there? To invite those from the retreat who are still in town and interested? I am keen to know what research has to say about this. And I have no hesitation in asking GP to do this research. Are you game, GP? Are you game, Riya? Is this of interest to both of you?'

There were vigorous nods and yeses all around. Sumit and Meena were sitting up straighter. The body language between the two had improved, and there was a sense of calmness though, of course, the wounds would take time to heal.

Gautam wanted to carry out the discussion in an outdoorsy kind of space. But we couldn't readily think of one. It was to be a conversation in the evening and finish with dinner. So, end of the day. It would cut down on the chance of conflicting schedules and a big rush to leave for other commitments or other work.

Somewhat shyly and hesitatingly, I asked Gautam and Riya if it was okay to do this at my home. I was certain of support from Manu. And of arranging the evening so that everyone was comfortable and easy. They were both rather happy with the suggestion. Yup, I could go ahead and do it. Manu would be happy to play host and have a chance to catch up with Gautam. And if we were going to discuss desire, romance and love and how to make the relationship better over the years, it would be just as well for him to be around for this discussion. Killing two birds with one stone and all that . . .

Riya called me later to confirm that nearly all of the twenty participants from the retreat would be there. This did not include Gautam and me, so the count was seriously high. Manu pitched in with his usual warm and hospitable style of hosting. And we were all set for the following Saturday evening.

I was energized and pumped. This was a clear goal that I knew I could achieve. There was work to be done at two levels. Strike that, three levels. My research on the topic. Making my home more presentable. And, of course, organizing the snacks, drinks and food. I would not serve anything alcoholic until the discussion was closed.

A day or two later, Riya called to say that the portal's founder and CEO would like to join us as well. Cool! I was excited to host him. His creation had been instrumental in bringing Manu and me together. If it weren't for the portal, chances are that we would never have met. Never found each other. Our personal and professional lives were very different. Our universes did not intersect at all and possibly would never have if not for the founder's brainwave of a matchmaking site.

I heard from Riya again a day later. The number of people had gone up as the head honcho was expected to attend. And because the number had gone up, the portal itself would arrange for a catered, full-service evening. I did not have to worry beyond my own research and the space. Hey! I had been looking forward to arranging a sumptuous dinner for everyone. Whatever!

It was finally Saturday. I had made arrangements to set up my living area with comfortable seating. The fairy lights and lovely, lush plants that Manu had made sure to arrange added to the glow and ambience of the evening. Over the past few days, Manu and I were closer and more intimate than we'd been in a while. We were united and working in tandem.

Their CEO was mellower and more unassuming than I had expected. His interest was visible, and his interactions with everyone present were cordial. He took the time to congratulate Manu and myself, and told us how delighted he was that we had matched on his platform. He had a thought or two about how we could share our story with a larger group of people and help the portal reach more and more people. About how we could encourage them with our story and others like ours.

Riya welcomed everyone and set the tone for the evening. 'Whether you've been married for nineteen years like Sumit and Meena or are not married yet, a common concern is keeping romance alive. Making sure the relationship remains vibrant and is not dulled by the passage of time. So that we continue to desire our partners months and years beyond the initial rush. Some of us had an impromptu meet-up last week and collectively decided to have this discussion.

'Gautam asked GP to research this, so she will first share her research, and then Gautam will engage us once more in a transformational discussion. Our founder and CEO is also here, making this evening extra-special. As is the fact that GP and Manu are hosting us. Well, folks, over to GP!'

This was something I enjoyed: a free flow of thoughts and words based on hard data and researched facts from many disciplines. 'I thought I would first ask all of you why it is important to be romantic. Now that you've been matched, married or partnered for a while, what difference does it make?

'Because research says . . . oh, forget research, our lives attest to the importance of being in love. To feel it. To experience romance. And to continue experiencing it.

'Romance is important because it makes us happier. It makes our partner happier. It helps us relate physically and enjoy sex more. It sparks all the excitement of the first meeting and the first few months. It adds more depth and meaning to our relationships. It wards off mental-health issues because you have someone who has your back. You have someone who is your safe space. Someone who hears you and pays attention. It boosts not only the immune system and longevity but also self-confidence and self-esteem, making you better at work and more productive. It reduces the chances of your partner cheating on you. You have more energy to focus on your career. It appears to simply be a way of getting more from life.

'I'll be brief and ask Gautam to help us understand how to keep the spark and desire alive after a few years of togetherness. Over to you, Gautam.'

Gautam was smiling as he stood and faced us. Turning to me, he said, 'GP, desire starts with you. It starts with nurturing yourself. Looking after yourself. Not just in fitness or grooming but in the nourishing attitude and actions you adopt in your own life. Just like the other brings out your best, and that is the feeling of loving the other, you need to bring out your best. You need to be dynamic and purposeful. Confident and immersed in whatever engages you.

> *Desire starts with you. It starts with nurturing yourself. Looking after yourself. Not just in fitness or grooming but in the nourishing attitude and actions you adopt in your own life.*

'When Manu and you met, both of you were at the top of your game. That's what the attraction was, wasn't it? The fact that you were both living life to the fullest—and not in the sometimes misunderstood way of living fully by working hard and partying hard. A full life is so much more.

'Tell me, tell us, GP, when your corporate career ended, did you or did you not get into a blue funk? You felt hopeless, and your confidence took a hard knock. How did that impact your relationship with yourself and with Manu? Think a bit about it. We become instantly more attractive to ourselves and our partner when we are purposeful, confident and engaged. You don't have to be uber-successful. You just have to be purposeful and confident.

'When you know who you are and have a plan to bring out your best, it brings a new zest to the relationship. And if both of you are like that, it is transformational. Remember always that the world sees us the way we see ourselves.'

> 'I think space gives spark. We long to meet each other. For us, travelling apart and travelling together keeps the spark alive. Sharing things and even a walk together keeps the spark alive. Keeping away from each other is very important because that is when you crave to be with each other.'
>
> —Shibani Kashyap (in a personal chat)

I was blown away by Gautam's observations. Yes, our relationship had dipped badly after the end of my corporate career. And cares and responsibilities had taken a huge toll, particularly on my physical and emotional health. A toll on my interactions and the quality of our relationship.

It all fell into place then. It was not the corporate thing but the fact that I was upset, at a low and experiencing a loss of confidence in myself. How could that low state have possibly been charming or attractive? Yes, I was not at my best at that time. Every time I was engaged and purposeful, I was instantly more attractive. I felt more attractive and took better care of myself. Physically, mentally and emotionally.

Take the last three to four weeks. Ever since the overseas retreat, the travel and putting together the whole shebang, I felt needed, relevant and meaningful. Not just as a caregiver, a wife or a mother, but in the area of my skills and for a larger purpose. Well-being and confidence once again coursed through my veins. It lifted my relationship with Manu to a higher plane of cordiality and desire. Being engaged and purposeful was a turn-on. Being in that state of purposefulness meant my romantic quotient was higher.

Perhaps it was not on my partner to turn me on. I needed to be on that plane to be turned on.

Gautam continued, 'GP has always been throwing up one definition after another. I have been fielding them. It is my turn today to quote from Dictionary.com. It assigns six meanings to intimacy. And includes in those six a close, familiar and usually affectionate or loving personal relationship with another person or group. And, of course, physical intimacy or sexual intercourse. It even says that intimacy is "a close association with or detailed knowledge or deep understanding of a place, subject, or period of history".'

Gautam continued, 'Physical intimacy is the easier one, isn't it? It is more difficult in a way to understand the other, that detailed knowledge or deep understanding. This is what true intimacy entails in being partnered, in marriage and in close relationships.

Increasing intimacy leads to greater connectedness, which leads to increased intimacy. Unite, but not just as parents talking about your responsibilities or what needs doing around the house. Unite as the friends, partners and lovers you also are.

'Like the moon, desire waxes and wanes. Increasing intimacy leads to greater connectedness, which leads to increased intimacy. Unite, but not just as parents talking about your responsibilities or what needs doing around the house. Unite as the friends, partners and lovers you also are. It all depends on what facets of your relationship you are focused on.

> 'We don't stop playing because we grow old, we grow old because we stop playing.'
>
> —George Bernard Shaw

'When you are purposeful, you are young and feel young. Your vibe is young. And isn't that so necessary when you want to increase romance and desire in your life? When do you feel old? When you have not nurtured yourself and given yourself time. If you feel attractive and pampered, you will automatically become more attractive to your partner.

If you feel attractive and pampered, you will automatically become more attractive to your partner.

'All the jokes about women liking successful and wealthy men have a grain of truth. The fact is that successful and wealthy men are purposeful and engaged. They are mentally youthful. Open to adventure and more willing to be spontaneous in life. Not weighed down with responsibilities and caregiving. Desire and romance are directly proportional to your feelings of self-worth. Self-worth is directly linked to how you feel about yourself. And how well you manage yourself.'

Desire and romance are directly proportional to your feelings of self-worth. Self-worth is directly linked to how you feel about yourself. And how well you manage yourself.

Riya spoke next: 'Not everyone is privileged, Gautam, and responsibilities are a fact of life. Chetan and I don't have kids right now, but we do take care of our parents and even younger siblings. We hope to be parents sometime. Married life will not be in isolation, nor are we rich enough, like in the example you just shared.'

Her CEO interjected, 'Riya, I think the point that Gautam has raised is totally different. He is talking about the approach. He is not pointing to anyone's net worth, nor is he talking about doing away with responsibilities and cares.

'He is simply pointing out the approach that can enhance romance and desire in a long-term partnership or marriage. And I guess what he is really saying is that it is enormously attractive to your partner when you are happy with who you are. When you are happy with your life.'

He had summed it up so well. The lingering silence seemed to embrace us all. Manu quietly slung his arm around me, whispering his deep appreciation of my research and speaking skills.

The long shadows of the evening were outside the circle of light. The catering service was unobtrusive as they went about setting the dining table and loading it with plates and flatware. The aromas from the kitchen beckoned. We were all ready to bring our A game to the dinner that awaited us.

'How to keep the spark alive? Keep the conversation going. Make the time to talk. EVERY DAY. Make time for each other. Without intrusion. Don't take your partner for granted. Acknowledge them and give your gratitude. I think it comes down to gratitude and surprise.'

—Padma Shri Dr Bibek Debroy (in a personal chat)

GAUTAM'S GUIDANCE

I was looking forward to hearing from Gautam on what would be the best way to keep the romance and even infatuation alive in my marriage. In all long-term partnerships and marriages.

But Gautam turned the tables on me. He demanded that I put my research to good use and define practical ways and means for putting into practice all that he had discussed. He thought I had enough material to do that. He wanted to see it in practical bullet points and insisted that I share it not only with the retreat participants, not only with the portal, but also with as many people as I could as a part of the paying it forward that he was also so insistent on.

I thought publishing his speech and transcribing notes from the evening would be enough. I racked my brains on ways to add to it and created a list— small, manageable and practical—that would help in bringing romance alive and fanning the embers of desire. In helping us want what we already have.

What emerged was how important it is to become a person with:

- Self-love and self-nurturing behaviour
- Physical activity and fitness. Physical awareness
- Engagement and purpose
- Confidence
- A sense of adventure and spontaneity in spirit and action
- A fondness for travel—alone and together

- Appreciation and attentiveness
- The ability to acknowledge and be kind to the other person
- The ability to not typecast the other. To rise above stereotypes
- To create time for togetherness and paying undivided attention

The savvy know that investing in romance is a smart move. The payback is enormous, as it lifts the quality of life of both partners and the family.

Some practical things to do:

- A flower a day for at least 100 days. Continue to remove those that wilt or wither.
- A bound journal with your entry for your partner. Every single day of the year. To be handed over on your anniversary or your partner's birthday. Priceless.
- Travel together (even if it is just for a night or two). Minus the kids.
- Travel without each other
- The weekly date night
- Cooking for the other
- Unexpected love notes and messages. Surprise them with your creativity and spontaneity.
- Getting to truly know the other person is intimacy at its finest
- Practise *1001 Ways To Be Romantic* by bestselling author on romance and relationships, Gregory J.P. Godek, or as many as appeal to you
- The unexpected vacation
- The unexpected 5-minute massage
- Appreciation, appreciation, appreciation
- Gratitude, gratitude, gratitude

- Think of more ways of surprising your partner and being more spontaneous
- Play together—a sport, flirt, party, feel good time, lighthearted time

The more grateful you are and the more appreciative you are of each other, the more desire will grow between you.

'Let there be spaces in your togetherness, And let the winds of the heavens dance between you. Love one another but make not a bond of love: Let it rather be a moving sea between the shores of your souls. Fill each other's cup but drink not from one cup. Give one another of your bread but eat not from the same loaf. Sing and dance together and be joyous, but let each one of you be alone, Even as the strings of a lute are alone though they quiver with the same music. Give your hearts, but not into each other's keeping. For only the hand of Life can contain your hearts. And stand together, yet not too near together: For the pillars of the temple stand apart, And the oak tree and the cypress grow not in each other's shadow.'

—Khalil Gibran (*The Prophet*)

THE FOUR BASES OF POWER

SATARA IDDHIPADA
(MANIFESTING AND ACHIEVING IN THE MODERN WORLD)

Iddhi (Pali) or *riddhi* (Sanskrit) means power or that which is potent. *Pada*, in both Pali and Sanskrit, refers to the base or foundation. Read together, it means the basis of power. In this case, mental power or as the Buddha likened it, spiritual power.

Spiritual power, you ask? What place does it have in a book about finding, keeping and nurturing romance? These bases of power are subtle. So consider this to be subtle power—power of the spirit. Spiritual power. That which brings us a step closer to manifesting our dreams and desires in the modern world.

In the *Viraddha Sutra* (*Sutta*) the Buddha is quoted as saying, 'Bhikkus, those who have neglected the four bases for spiritual power have neglected the noble path leading to the complete destruction of suffering.'

The four bases of power apply equally in the modern world to our lives in our quest to become happy and progress. These can be applied to any goal in life. Based on my lived experience, these four bases are also the means of manifesting what we desire and bringing it about.

The four bases are:

Intention (*chanda*)
Effort (*viriya*)
Consciousness (*citta*)
Investigation (*vimamsa* in Pali and *mimamsa* in Sanskrit)

Chanda is subtle. It is intent. It is purpose. It is passion. It is the singlemindedness or determination to achieve a goal. It is an intense desire. Without *chanda*, there is no beginning to any quest. With it, the path becomes clear, and our energy is correctly focused. It takes intense determination to achieve what we set out to do. In the matter of finding a partner, intent is key. In the matter of creating a happy life together, intent is key. It is our decision and our communication with the universe.

This wholehearted desire to attain, reach, fulfil or accomplish a certain task is a concentration. Because only when our intent is concentrated can it help us persevere. To persevere in the face of obstacles and distractions that are inevitable in any journey or quest. Today, time is the biggest obstacle. When too much time elapses **after** we have set our intention and started to make the effort, we are easily discouraged. And start to doubt. It is then that the concentration of intention is needed. Otherwise, there would be little difference between the power of intention and a wish or a daydream.

Concentrated or intense desire can either be wholesome or unwholesome. Remember that the Buddha did not label things as right or wrong. But as helpful or unhelpful. Helpful and wholesome desire is called *kusala chanda*. That intense desire, which does not stem from greed. That which is free of greed is termed *alobha* (without greed). Wholesome desire does not carry hatred, animosity or rage and therefore it is not hateful (*adosa*). And the desire is not delusional (*amoha*).

And so it follows that unhelpful, unwholesome desire is *akusala chanda* and either stems from or is tainted by *lobha* (greed), *dosa* (animosity or hatred) and *moha* (delusion).

The second power is that of our old friend. Effort or *viriya*. Heroic effort, effort in the right direction, and the energy to persist. To follow through. Interestingly enough, here is a viriya with different stages of effort. The effort to start or to begin is *aramba dhatu viriya*. The effort to sustain in spite

When what we desire does not reveal itself, when progress appears to have stagnated, we give in to doubt and the fatigue of the effort so far.

of obstacles is *nikkama dhatu viriya*. And finally, the effort to continue till completion, which is *parakkam dhatu viriya*.

The Buddha recognized that effort varies, just like desire effort too ebbs and flows. We have all experienced a relatively easy and passionate start to a project or something new. It has momentum and energy. And drive. Sustaining something over time and continuing with the effort despite obstacles, doubt and uncertainty is the true test of our intention and our ability to persevere.

Time tests us and our patience. When what we desire does not reveal itself, when progress appears to have stagnated, we give in to doubt and the fatigue of the effort so far. This is what the Buddha experienced before attaining enlightenment. This is human experience with manifestation. This is the human experience of life. Effort becomes heroic because it persists until it wins. Until the quest is fulfilled.

Effort becomes heroic because it persists until it wins. Until the quest is fulfilled.

Citta is another name for consciousness. For the mind. It embraces human mental faculties. The world of feelings and thoughts. The concentration of the mind is its spiritual power. Why? We accept easily that distracted driving is the cause of accidents. A distraction of mere seconds can be fatal. To oneself or another.

The disturbed mind does not allow for progress. It is scattered. The concentration of the mind is about bringing to bear our mindful and complete focus, mindfulness and awareness to the task at hand.

Without mindfulness, we cannot observe or know what is important to our partner. We will be oblivious to not just a birthday or anniversary but to what is truly important to them. What brings them joy. What disturbs them. And how to demonstrate our love. Our appreciation and awareness of them.

Without mindfulness, we are unaware of even our innermost motives and our intent. We have not examined ourselves, our lives and our determinations.

There are three elements to *citta*. The first is *citta* itself or consciousness. The second is that of *samadhi* or deep concentration. Single-minded focus. And finally, our ability to consciously strive and move in the right direction, to direct our efforts. Without mindfulness, the third one is not possible. This conscious striving is *padhana sankhara*.

The last power is that of investigation or discrimination. Referred to either as *vimamsa* or *mimamsa*. The English equivalent is investigation, reasoning, analysis or wisdom. Deep questioning and examination. Perhaps understanding or a wise understanding based on analysis and reasoning.

These four bases of power are among the thirty-seven conditions or requisites of enlightenment. As the Buddha said, 'Bhikhus, there are these four bases of spiritual power that, when cultivated and often developed, lead to going from the near shore to the far shore.'

'For example, the journey from Kamakura to Kyoto takes twelve days. If you travel for eleven but stop with only one day remaining, how can you admire the moon over the capital?'

—Nichiren Daishonin,
13th-century Japanese sage

HAPPILY EVER AFTER

STILL MY INSIDE JOB

> 'I have seen no other cause than the
> presence of correct views to inspire right
> thoughts in the mind and to improve the
> right thoughts already present in the mind.'
>
> —The Buddha (*The Numerical Discourses*)

For some time, I had this strange feeling inside. One of sadness, as though something bad was going to happen. Something inside me seemed to be waiting for it.

Each doorbell ring and each ring of the phone felt like a jolt, like a taser to my stretched nerves. And for those two weeks, nothing seemed to be able to distract me. Not my walks, affirmations or any amount of journalling. Oh sure, it worked for that duration, and then I was back to the nail-biting, nervous feeling in the pit of my stomach.

For some reason, my first meeting with Gautam was uppermost in my mind. I had even dreamed of it. Other vignettes kept forming in my mind's eye. At times, I could see him standing on a road in the blazing sun of a midsummer afternoon. And this was something that really had not happened between us. But it was clear enough to feel real. As though it **had** happened at some time, somewhere. In other dreams, I could feel his tap on my shoulder and see him holding his palm out to me with money on it. And, so many times, I felt I was at the Tea Shoppe, listening to him with every fibre of my being. His words to me that I must help others kept echoing in my mind.

What was I sensing? What did it portend? What was going to happen?

Gautam's number flashing on my phone was both soothing and unexpected. The conversation left me stunned. Bereft. What on earth . . . Gautam's voice still ringing in my ears. He wanted to meet me. One last time for now, he said. He would not be around for some time.

Last time? What? Not going to be around for some time? What did he mean? He was going away, but for how long? And how did he think I would manage without him?

I was still upset at not receiving the kind of corporate opportunity I was seeking. I felt defunct without my professional identity. Without the purposefulness of a full day. Without much of a direction. How would I even begin to find my purpose? I needed Gautam to find direction once more in life. The void in my life—I needed his sage counsel to fill it. For him to tell me what to do. And what about helping others? For the moment, I wasn't even helping myself. How would I help anyone else?

Only a face-to-face meeting would help us resolve this. Manu, too, was shocked. He had gone quiet on hearing that Gautam would be leaving us for now. He said, 'I owe Gautam a great debt of gratitude. If you are meeting him this week, I would like to join you. Do you also want to invite some of your friends who've met him earlier? I distinctly remember you telling me about so many others who'd met him earlier and benefited from it. Would you like to host them? It could be a farewell for Gautam with a small group of people. We can have them all over for lunch or dinner.'

It was such a great idea, but I hesitated for a bit. Perhaps I ought to meet with Gautam by myself. I needed to come to terms with him not being around for some time. Or was I being too selfish? If Manu felt so deeply about meeting Gautam, then I had to expand my own wants and needs to include his. I did know that whoever in my circle of friends had met and interacted with Gautam over the years would have liked to meet him and bid him well on his next adventure. Whatever it was.

So much had changed over the years. My dearest friend, Rajiv Churamani, was no more. His untimely demise was a huge blow to me. He had been unfailingly supportive and a great friend in the most difficult years of my life. He had Gautam's wisdom and something close to Gautam's perspective. His sage counsel had been my support through those difficult years. I owed so much to Rajiv. Reema and Vikram were now based in England. Even Aparna and Harsh were now in Bangalore. But they were willing to come to town and bid a fond farewell to Gautam.

Within two days, it was all set. The guest list was comprehensive: Superna, Aparna and Harsh, Shachi, Chirag, Prashant, Sudip Sehgal and unsurprisingly, Riya, Sumit and Meena from the first retreat. And yes, there were conversations and mails happening about the next or even a series of retreats. What would happen to them, I wondered? Tulika, as usual, wouldn't be able to make it as she was busy.

We would meet over dinner at my place. Gautam always preferred it if people were not in a rush, which automatically made dinner the right choice. As it meant that everyone would be present and not be in a hurry to end the meeting and get on with the next thing on their agenda.

Knowing Gautam, everyone made it a point to be on time. And I had been savvy enough to give Gautam a slightly later time. Manu and I had both felt that it would be a wonderful thing to have everyone there ahead of Gautam. We could all welcome him together. The hugs, the bonhomie, the warmth. I felt my eyes welling up again and again. Manu came over and slid his arm around me for a few precious moments, hugging me to his side. Comfort and a spot of courage.

The conversation was settling down and centred on Gautam. We all knew him and wanted to be with him as much as possible. The light music was the perfect accompaniment to the flowing conversation of the evening. The initial rush for a drink and something to eat was somehow more controlled and almost missing. The tone of the evening was filled with both quiet happiness and the calmness that was so much a part of Gautam's aura.

Somehow, we all formed a semi-circle around Gautam. It seemed that the evening had taken on a life of its own. Magical. Quiet. Serene. I could feel the desire to make the most of Gautam's presence in our midst. Superna's slightly whiny staccato did not take me by surprise when she said, 'Gautam, I am meeting you after sometime. We have met many times since I first met you at GP's house those years ago. I have always done whatever you asked me to do. Just like GP. But she has succeeded, and I have not. I have not found anyone, and now that I am over 50, I don't expect to either. So did you give GP a secret mantra? What went wrong in my case? I am really curious'.

Whoa . . . somehow, I had been reluctant to invite Superna. Her old patterns of complaints had never really dissolved. But for Manu's insistence on inviting all those who had interacted with Gautam, I would have left her off the guest list. Besides, she had not bothered to meet me and offer her condolences when my dad passed away. This was despite the fact that she had known him for a long time and that he had tried his best to help her with a police matter when her house was robbed. I found it hard to give up on that bit of resentment within. Just a WhatsApp message of condolence did not really cut it. Not to speak of my own friendship with her for so many years and all my efforts to help her with various things. I had done my best to help her.

Gautam was calm as he said, 'But would you say you are happier now than when we first met, Superna? Not really fully content but somewhat happier than earlier?'

'Yes, I am,' Superna replied. 'But I really, really want to know why something that has worked for so many others has not worked well for me. Where did it all go wrong?'

> *If you live your life well and embrace your singlehood, you will evolve. Which is exactly what partnering with another person does.*

'Well, Superna, first of all, you must truly accept that not having a romantic partner does not limit your life. If you live your life well and embrace your singlehood, you will evolve. Which is exactly what partnering with another person does. Connections are possible everywhere. Once you understand this, you can expand your life. You can celebrate your life.

'And there really is no comparison with someone else. GP followed through and evolved. It all depends on how hard we are willing to work on ourselves. And how wisely we choose. Many times, people tend to be bad at knowing what will bring them happiness and what they want from a relationship. So they may well end up not accepting a boyfriend who is not ideal-looking. They may choose a better-looking partner over someone who is hard-working. Or someone who has an addictive personality over someone who is light-hearted and flirts at parties. Or someone who is not approved by society.

'People looking for a life partner must have both deep wisdom and flexibility. Some people get stuck on ticking off a checklist and finding someone who checks all the boxes. We don't give people a chance. We don't give ourselves a chance when we don't grow and use our wisdom to be flexible in our choices.

'Isn't it interesting that research shows that the more someone wants a relationship, the less satisfied they will be with their life in the absence of it? One of the things that GP did was that she did not allow the rest of life to stop. She continued living and

> *Research shows that the more someone wants a relationship, the less satisfied they will be with their life in the absence of it.*

> *You have to be happy with who you are before you start looking for a partner.*

living well. I have always said that you have to be happy with who you are before you start looking for a partner.

'Many people get stuck in the pursuit of the one. They may forget that someone becomes the one by what they do. Someone may not be exactly right or exactly the one. But he or she may have the potential to be a wonderful partner, a wonderful companion and a wonderful friend.

'After all, people enter into relationships for the long term. Studies show that 86 per cent of young people assume their current or future marriage will last forever. No one is entering into marriage for the short term. And yet, so many people choose a partner with a short-term focus or for the wrong reasons. With wisdom, you are able to choose someone who is definitely good to you and someone who is good for you. This last may not always be comfortable, but it will work to help you grow as a person.'

Manu surprised me by speaking up and even more with what he had to say: 'I agree with you, Gautam. When I met GP, she was truly living life well. Self-reliant, independent and professionally successful. She was able to turn her life around with your advice, and kudos to the enormous effort she put in and for not giving up. She **was** happy and thriving. Not waiting for marriage as a solution to her problems.

'And that training—your training—has continued. Life has not been easy over the last few years. But she has been resilient and forward-looking through painful circumstances and difficulties.'

Everything appeared blurry through my tear-filled eyes. I hurried to the kitchen under the pretext of checking on the food. I returned a few minutes later when I had gathered myself. I was just in time to hear Gautam ask Sudip Sehgal, 'Well, Sudip, how are you doing? And in the context of the conversation with Superna, how are you managing your singlehood?'

The tall and good-looking Sudip replied, 'Gautam, I am honest with myself about where I went wrong. I did not manage my expectations well. Because I have been overseas, I have not interacted with you as much as everyone else here, but the one key takeaway for me since I met you so many years ago is that it is important to evolve as an individual to be happy.

'As someone who has never been married, I think it is equally important to make peace with it or come to terms with it.

'And even now, I feel that single people get left out of family and friends' functions. And your parents still don't take you seriously because you are not married. Somehow, I feel that the element of respect is missing.'

Many of the others stepped up to disabuse Sudip of this notion. But there **was** a grain of truth in it. Society has its own notions of how life ought to be lived.

Riya said, slowly and reflectively, 'I think Gautam, what you just said a few minutes ago is the ultimate advice. Work on yourself to become a better person, and by doing that, you enrich the relationship. You become the right person for that partnership and for marriage. We are all so focused on the other person—finding the right person, marrying the right person, and even questioning our choice when something does not go right. For me, this is a new thought—to become the right person for a relationship.'

> *Work on yourself to become a better person, and by doing that, you enrich the relationship. You become the right person for that partnership and for marriage. We are all so focused on the other person—finding the right person, marrying the right person, and even questioning our choice when something does not go right.*

Gautam was smiling as he answered Riya in his courteous way: 'In the modern world, there is a tendency to see your companion, your partner and your mate only in terms of their rightness. And their being right depends so much on what they are giving you—whether they are giving you what you want or what you need. Marriage is not a means of wish fulfilment. Your partner is not just a provider. Yes, they are a provider beyond just the financial. But not merely so. Marriage is a means of continuing your evolution and growing the boundaries of your inner self, your heart and your life.

'We ask people who are recently married, "How is married life treating you?" No one thinks of asking, "How are you and your partner treating the relationship?" The answer to that is key to the state of the relationship. Are you approaching the relationship from your heart?'

'Marriage is about conversation. A happy joyous friendship! For me, the cornerstone of love is friendship. I wanted a person I could grow with and look up to. Marriage is not about the tangible but about things that are intangible like conversation, laughter and friendship.'

—Nisha JamVwal (in a personal chat)

Shachi said, 'That is so wise, Gautam. Truly, no one stops to ask how we are treating our relationship. Sometimes we treat it well, and then other times we fall back on our ego. Sometimes it is genuinely about our partner, and other times it is only about ourselves. Of course, having children changes the equation. I could truly support my husband in following his dreams, but once we had our children, it was more about them and much less about us.'

Chetan edged in closer and said, 'Compatibility is really tested by children. I met my wife only after I started following Gautam's guidance. We have been very compatible throughout, but our major stress comes from our children not listening to us or not doing well. I think we are very good parents, but as with all working couples, we end up parenting on the fly. And when I say no to either of the girls, my wife doesn't like it.

'On the other hand, I find that she has a soft corner for the elder one and simply doesn't allow me to discipline the kids the way I think is necessary. It is a huge strain on our bond. I don't know what the answer or solution to this is. For quite some time, I've been thinking of reaching out to you, Gautam. I was so shocked when GP called and invited me to see you off today. I feel I am perhaps meeting you a bit too late. But please, please tell me what I should do as a parent and husband. I assure you that I would never have missed out on being here this evening. I am not here just for this ulterior motive of seeking your guidance, you know.'

There was amusement all around. Chetan's voice was pleading and cajoling. It was amply clear to all of us that the discord at home had been on his mind. Just as his sincerity in being there was clear. He truly wished to bid farewell to Gautam along with the rest of us, even though we all hoped this absence would be temporary.

The platters of snacks were getting cold and drinks were languishing unattended. I was fielding impatient signals from my staff. They were wondering what to do with the rotation of snacks. Signalling them to hold their horses, I continued in my safe spot close to Manu. He, too, had forgotten to play host for the moment. We were all focused on Gautam and what he had to say. Chetan's concern struck a common chord with many of us.

Gautam said, 'And you have, of course, tried talking about this with your wife, I am sure. You feel you have not succeeded. Have you asked your wife what her point of view is? Have you asked her to give you a solution? Have you listened when she has tried to explain her point of view to you? We often listen half-heartedly. We are so eager to rush in with our point of view that our listening is unfair. We are unfair to each other, and ultimately, we are unfair to our relationship.

'We are convinced about how right and knowledgeable we are. This automatically puts the other person down. It is very easy to lose respect and to lose sight of the other person's contributions to our lives. To our partnership. Because we are so much closer to our own point of view. We know our contribution to the relationship more intimately. We know what we do and our intent for the partnership more intimately.

'The spotlight is on the wrong end of the stage. Reverse it, I say. Put the spotlight on each other. Ask your partner to share their point of view. Even their dreams and hopes for the future. Solutions will emerge. The two of you will be stronger than the stress of raising children together. You are a team. You need to understand that you will still be together when your children are grown and have moved out of the house. Cement your understanding of each other to strengthen the bonds between you. Without the right understanding of the other person, their motivations, and what prompts them to be a certain way and do certain things, you lack intimacy.'

Here, Gautam broke off and looked at me with his charming smile. Everyone knew he was referring to my single-minded focus on the topic of intimacy during the recently concluded retreat. I had to put up with some good-natured leg-pulling over this.

Time was slipping away, and I was keen to make sure that Gautam and all the guests ate well. With Gautam, I always took extra care since he did not eat very late in the evenings. Questions and queries would continue. I racked my brains for the one last thing that would satisfy everyone.

And so I asked Gautam, 'What is the one thing that you would give us today by way of suggestion, Gautam? The one thing that will make a difference in our lives. To our partners and our lives together. I don't want to rush anyone, but please let this be the last question of the evening. You all know that if Gautam does not eat now, he will skip his dinner altogether.'

Gautam took a few moments to think and said, 'Knowing yourself and your partner well is key to experiencing appreciation and gratitude. Appreciation and gratitude lead to respect. Respect is acceptance, not expectation. Acceptance strengthens the feelings of affection and the bond between the partners.

'Don't compare your partner to past partners, others' partners or whatever the Internet or culture portrays as the ideal. Continue to take responsibility for your own fulfilment at every stage of life. At every stage of the partnership.

'If I had to leave one method behind with you, it would be the loving kindness meditation of the Buddha. *Karuna-mitta* or the *mitta-bhavna* benevolence meditation.

'Sit quietly, upright and alone, and gently focus on your breath. Begin by blessing yourself. Moving from yourself to those you love, those you are neutral about, and finally, those you actively dislike. Wish each one well. Focus your attention again on yourself and say to yourself, "May I be well and happy. May I be peaceful and calm. May I be at ease. May I be protected from danger. May I be safe. May my mind be free of hatred. May my heart be filled with love. May I be well and happy." This is only a suggested script. You can always write your own script. And keep changing it with a change in life and your outlook.

'Your script can be in a notebook. Write it brightly and boldly. Say it in a gentle, murmured repetition of the words rather than silently.

'With this, become more accepting of who you are and of those around you.'

The silence continued even after Gautam stopped speaking. The only sound was that of the air-conditioning and the clatter of plates and cutlery being put on the dining table.

Gautam had equipped us with the tools, and now it was up to us to take them forward in our lives and help others as well.

A germ of an idea had been brewing. While looking at Gautam chatting with others, his words of nearly sixteen years ago were echoing once again in my mind: 'Help others once you are helped.' I was indebted to him forever. I had found love and understood partnership with another person because of him.

Perhaps I could write about whatever I had experienced and whatever Gautam had shared with me. It was the only way I could think of that would help others. Perhaps a book, or even two. Who knew where this desire to help others, as I had once been helped by Gautam, would lead? I could see light breaking over the horizon of my life. Yet again, it was time for a fresh start. Yet again, I would seize the moment.

'Who you marry, which is the ultimate partnership, is enormously important in determining your happiness in life and your success and I was lucky in that respect.'

—Warren Buffet (not in a personal chat)

REFERENCES

Two books that remain central to the writing of this book are Dr Daisaku Ikeda's *Discussions on Youth*, Volume 1, and *The Living Buddha: An Interpretive Biography*. I also referred throughout to several writings of Nichiren Daishonin from *Writings of Nichiren Daishonin*, Volume I.

I would like my readers to know that I have read over several hundred views in over a hundred books and articles of Dr Daisaku Ikeda on life, karma and the philosophy of Nichiren Daishonin. This includes his writings on relationships, family, human revolution (continuous person growth) and many others.

A non-exhaustive list of sources:
The Buddha In Your Mirror by Woody Hochswender, Greg Martin and Ted Marino.

Buddha and the Gospel of Buddhism by Ananda K. Coomaraswamy

Buddhist Scriptures by Edward Conze

Buddhism in a New Light by Shin Yatomi

Magic By Rhonda Bryne

Great Disciples of the Buddha by Nyanaponika Thera & Hellmuth Hecker

The Buddha—A Short Biography by John S. Strong

Marriage by Devdutt Pattanaik

Buddha by Karen Armstrong

The Life and Times of the Buddha, Shree Book Center

Power, Freedom and Grace by Deepak Chopra

The Little Prince, by Antoine De Saint Exupery

The Happiness Advantage by Shawn Achor

The Life of Buddha and its Lessons by HS Olcott

What the Buddha Taught by Walpola Sri Rahula

Many Mansions by Gina Cerminara

If the Buddha Dated by Charlotte Kasl

The Seven Principles for Making Marriage Work by John. M. Gottman and Nan Silver

A Book for Couples by Hugh and Gayle Prather

Get the Guy by Matthew Hussey

The Buddha's teachings on Prosperity by Bhikkhu Basnagoda Rahula

The Science of Happily Ever After, TY Tashiro

Why Buddhism? by Vicki Mackenzie

Why Buddhism Is True by Robert Wright

Desperately Seeking Shah Rukh by Shrayana Bhattacharya

366 Gems from Buddhism by Robert Van de Weyer

Buddhism 101 by Arnie Kozak

Sayings of the Buddha Oxford World's Classics

In the Buddha's Words by Bhikku Bodhi

The sources used for the duties of husband and wife are:
1. The Buddha's Teachings on Prosperity (cited above)
2. A dissertation on Early Buddhist interpersonal ethics: a study of the Singalovada Suttanta and its contemporary relevance, Clasquin-Johnson, Michel (https://uir.unisa.ac.za/handle/10500/17893)

References to Mara (outside of the writings of Dr Daisaku Ikeda) are from:
1. Britannica.com
2. www.learnreligions.com by Barbara O'Brien
3. Ananda WP Guruge, *The Buddha's Encounters with Mara the Tempter*

References to Klesha or Unskillful Emotions:
1. Online references from the Abhidhamma Pitaka Vibhaga
2. Online references from the Sutta Pitaka
3. www.learnreligions.com by Barbara O'Brien

ACKNOWLEDGEMENTS

My love for reading and writing, my obsession with books is my inheritance from my father, Birbal Nath. He passed away in 2016, a few months before my previous book, *Buddha at Work*, was first published. Books will always remind me of my dad, and he continues to be an integral, intrinsic part of my life.

My mother, Toshi Nath, held fast to her conviction that I have great potential and that one day I would somehow evolve or express it. And this despite the many disasters of my life—emotional and academic! Twenty-six years of separation have not eased the pain of her untimely demise.

It was Vuneeta Sarrin's compassion that made her reach out to me at life's nadir, a time of a hopelessness and helplessness. Her introduction of Nichiren Buddhism in my life in February 2000 was a turning point. Words cannot express my gratitude to her for this.

I am deeply grateful to the tireless efforts of Dr Daisaku Ikeda in spreading the practice of hope—Nichiren Daishonin's teachings have been transformational not just for me but for millions. The debt of gratitude to my mentor, Dr Ikeda, and the Sangha of the Bharat Soka Gakkai is one I will never be able to repay.

My writing is my humble contribution in paying forward the help I have received from my practice of the Daishonin's teachings in the Sangha of the Gakkai, made possible only because of Dr Daisaku Ikeda.

Meeting Manu was truly magical. The moment of our meeting is etched forever in my heart. To him I owe a tremendous debt—of walking life's path with me, through all that we have endured. He embodies a sense of responsibility like no one I have ever met. His sense of humour has stood the test of 17 years of marriage! And he still manages to make me laugh. Without Manu the Sangha of the family was not possible. I am eternally grateful to him.

To Padma Shri Dr Bibek Debroy, Raga D'Silva, Hiten Tejwani, Sudip Sehgal and Naveena Reddi I owe grateful thanks for the time and trouble they took to answer my questions and for their consent to be quoted. Shibani Kashyap was forthright and forthcoming over many voice notes and my gratitude to her. After reading Jeffrey Archer's *A Twist in the Tale*, I longed to meet Nisha JamVwal. Just listening to her life story from 10 p.m. till 1.30 a.m. on a night in June 2022 was a pleasure and a treasure of life lessons. Thanks are due to Sumita Mehta for her care, affection and time.

It took 22-year-old Sahil Sharma to understand why I wanted to and was, in fact, capable of writing *Buddha in Love*. Thank you, Sahil, for being there, and you are simply the best!

It was Nigel Yorwerth who took my literary work to an international readership, and I truly owe him a debt of gratitude for having done that. Thank you, Nigel, for the multiple international and language editions.

Team Penguin Random House is part of this journey. Gratitude to Milee Ashwarya, publisher, for accepting the very different concept of *BIL*. Thank you, Nicholas Rixon, for setting the ball rolling. Thank you, Saksham Garg, and I hope *BIL* answers the question you had asked—what qualifies me to write a book on love! Saksham, a big thank you for your tremendous support through the most difficult year of my life—2022!

Thanks all the way to Dipanjali Chadha for her patience, kindness and support. No one could have had a better editor. Thanks are due to the fabulous work done by Saloni Mital on the copy and the compelling questions to the author.

Among other friends who have supported my journey are Tulika S., Tikli Basu, Harpreet Kkaur and Siddharth Singh Rathore. Thanks for putting up with my endless calls and requests.

My good friend Uma Suresh Prabhu shared her thoughts on love and relationships with me and influenced mine. Thank you so much.

Many other people shared their views and thoughts with me. I have witnessed tears, laughter, hopelessness, despair and completion in equal measure. Grateful to them all.

Deepest gratitude to you, dear reader, for choosing *Buddha in Love* and being a part of my journey and making me a part of yours. Be well and be in love!